RETHINKING EDUCATION

Whose knowledge is it anyway?

About the authors

Adam Unwin is a Senior Lecturer in Education at the Institute of Education, University College London. His main work has been in London as a teacher and teacher educator. He is currently program leader for the Master of Teaching (MTeach), a course specifically for practising teachers. Research interests include new teacher learning, the role of technology in education, work-related learning and global development education. Adam has worked on various education projects in the UK and overseas. His postgraduate work includes an MSc in Development Studies and a Doctorate in Education. He has been an active trade unionist throughout his career.

John Yandell taught in London secondary schools for 20 years before moving to the Institute of Education, University College London, where he has worked since 2003. He is the editor of the journal *Changing English*, and the author of *The Social Construction of Meaning: reading literature in urban English classrooms* (Routledge, 2013). Other recent publications include *Critical Practice in Teacher Education: a study of professional learning*, which he co-edited with Ruth Heilbronn. He edited *Socialist Teacher* for 12 years and contributes regularly to *Education for Liberation*. Like Adam, he has been an active trade unionist throughout his working life.

Acknowledgements

We would like to thank British Museum staff and Anton Franks for sharing their ideas and collaborating with Adam on the 'cultures in contact' project that features in this book. Our appreciation to Sophie Herxheimer for her ongoing creative ideas and suggestions. Thanks to Ken Jones, David Lambert, Adrian Mee and Claire Armitstead for their very helpful comments on drafts. Thanks, too, to Chris Brazier for his editorial skill – and for his patience. The errors that remain are our own.

About the New Internationalist

New Internationalist is an award-winning, independent media co-operative. Our aim is to inform, inspire and empower people to build a fairer, more sustainable planet.

We publish a magazine on global-justice issues and a range of books, both distributed worldwide. We have a vibrant online presence and run ethical online shops for our customers and other organizations.

- **Independent media:** we're free to tell it like it is – our only obligation is to our readers and the subjects we cover.

- **Fresh perspectives:** our in-depth reporting and analysis provide keen insights, alternative perspectives and positive solutions for today's critical global justice issues.

- **Global grassroots voices:** we actively seek out and work with grassroots writers, bloggers and activists across the globe, enabling unreported (and under-reported) stories to be heard.

NONONSENSE

RETHINKING EDUCATION

Whose knowledge is it anyway?

Adam Unwin
and
John Yandell

New Internationalist

NONONSENSE
Rethinking Education
Whose knowledge is it anyway?

Published in 2016 by
New Internationalist Publications Ltd
The Old Music Hall
106-108 Cowley Road
Oxford OX4 1JE, UK
newint.org

Cover design: Juha Sorsa
Design concept: Andrew Smith, asmithcompany.co.uk

Series editor: Chris Brazier
Series design by Juha Sorsa

Printed and bound in Great Britain by Bell & Bain Ltd, Glasgow
who hold environmental accreditation ISO 14001.

MIX
Paper from
responsible sources
FSC® C007785

British Library Cataloguing-in-Publication Data.
A catalogue record for this book is available from the British Library.

Library of Congress Cataloging-in-Publication Data.
A catalog for this book is available from the Library of Congress.

ISBN 978-1-78026-309-0
(ISBN ebook 978-1-78026-310-6)

Contents

Foreword

Schools and schooling have become so commonplace in the Global North that we rarely question the fundamental assumptions supporting contemporary education. Of course, we seem eager for change: waves of educational 'reform' seek to improve our schools, make our children smarter, boost the economy, and create a just, enlightened society. But never are the founding conventions of modern schooling challenged in the public debates about education, and never do the schools change significantly. Instead, our constant anxiety about education is eased by promises of higher standards, more stringent testing, greater accountability, and increased rigor – that is, by promises to augment rather than truly reform the basic practices of education. This book sets out to make education strange to us by exposing the historical and contemporary forces that have invisibly shaped our notions of normal schooling. In so doing, it offers hope for a truly profound re-imagination of education.

As authors Unwin and Yandell demonstrate, the commonplace realities of education are easily rendered absurd by stepping back from the ordinary to take a critical perspective. Consider, for example, the material conditions of too many schools: drab, factory-like buildings set apart from their surrounding communities, with which they have little or no interaction; bland individual classrooms with their rows of desks and scant resources; the regulated routines of daily life (the bells, timed lessons, and work schedules); the physical segregation by age, ability, subject area, and activity.

Consider, too, what transpires within those structures: the assembly-line model of transmission education in which the subject of history, for example, is reduced to particles of information – eras, kings, wars – and delivered to children in ever larger but always disembodied chunks as they move through the system and the ever-increasing assessment regimes that mirror industrial quality control. These are not environments for unfettered exploration, serendipity, trial-and-error, social interaction, innovation, false starts, or passion, all of which distinguish the richest moments of teaching and learning.

Another absurdity is exposed when in-school instruction is compared to out-of-school instruction. Studies of situated and informal learning – some referenced by Unwin and Yandell – contrast *just-in-case teaching and learning* with *just-in-time teaching and learning*. The former is preparation for some imagined or anticipated future, and defines much formal schooling. The curricula and pedagogy for just-in-case teaching and learning assume that students will need a particular skill or knowledge set when they are examined, or when they move on to the next grade level, to secondary school, university, or the workplace. Here knowledge is seen as an accumulation of information that lies in wait for the appropriate moment of application.

In contrast, just-in-time teaching and learning occur in the context of and simultaneous with activities that immediately require the knowledge and skills being introduced. Such teaching and learning is typical in the workplace or other out-of-school settings, where they are linked to activities that are complex, collaborative and authentic, and that require not the isolated performance of individuals but, instead, the co-ordinated efforts of pairs or groups. In such circumstances, evaluation is also immediate, as the outcomes or effects of teaching and learning are instantly apparent. As Unwin and Yandell make clear, such spontaneity, co-operation, and excitement can also be created in schools, but only if we do some serious rethinking and revise some of the basic principles on which schooling is built.

What would a school based on these principles look like? It would be a hive of dialogue and activity, with individuals and small groups working in co-ordinated action across projects. Those projects would develop on different time scales, so that some might last years while others lasted days. Teachers and students would work into and with the community, and schools themselves would be the center of social activities that benefitted that community. Emphasis would be on the knowledge needed to achieve success at tasks, and evaluation would be conducted collectively and constantly as reflection on work done together.

Utopian aspirations, perhaps, but why settle for less? And an achievable Utopia, if we begin with the critique offered by this thoughtful and thought-provoking book. Unwin and Yandell offer a bleak picture of the ways in which social and economic forces have worked to produce mis-shapen schools, but they also provide a rich set of ideas on which a new school might be built, and they offer examples of what that might look like. The book should be read carefully and shared widely.

Anthony Paré
Professor of Language and Literacy Education
University of British Columbia
Canada

Introduction

Education is a huge and contested field – a field in which everyone has first-hand experience and a wealth of opinions, often largely based on those experiences. Being human involves learning – learning about the world in which we live, learning about ourselves and other people, learning how to survive and thrive. And most readers of this book will have had some experience of formal education: in some shape or form, we expect that you will have 'done school', and you may even feel that the time you spent in school has shaped who you are. People talk about what helped them to learn, and what hindered them, what subjects they found interesting or boring, which teachers they liked or disliked, and why. People come with ideas and beliefs about education in general and schooling in particular, and these beliefs are often so deeply ingrained, so personal, that it can be hard to scrutinize or challenge them: they appear as plain common sense.

In this book, our main focus is on schools and schooling. This isn't because we are not interested in preschool or university education – and we certainly don't believe that schools are the only places where education happens. Many of the issues covered in this book apply equally to other phases or sectors of education, and are also applicable to the learning that happens outside any institutional context. But we focus on the phases of formal education that most people (globally) are likely to experience.

We recognize that these experiences will be very different. A high school in an affluent urban area of Canada will be very different from a rural school in Nicaragua – different in the number of pupils, in the diversity of its intake, in the size of its classes, in the resources available. Differences in schooling reflect and reproduce differences in the societies that the schools serve. These differences are material as well as cultural. There is thus not a single model of schooling across the globe, or even within a single locality. And there are seldom simple, universally applicable solutions to educational problems. Even small schools are complicated and busy places – places in which multiple interests collide.

We want you to be able to engage fully – and critically – in the debates around education. What is the purpose or function of schools? Whose interests do they serve? How are resources allocated? Is education a route to empowerment and liberation, or is it a means of control? Are schools engines of social mobility or social justice, or merely tools that reproduce the inequalities of existing social and economic structures? Are schools beacons of hope, or prison-houses of the mind? What is the relationship between the formal education that is accomplished through schooling and the learning that happens in homes, communities and workplaces?

Much public discourse treats the goals and meanings of education as entirely unproblematic. But does everyone really agree on what a good school looks like? Or on how teachers and schools should be held accountable to the wider society? Is equality in education simply a matter of school places, or of fair and equal access to the same knowledge, the same curriculum, the same qualifications? Our aim in writing this book is to open up these questions about education – and to enable you to scrutinize and contest the easy claims that are often made by politicians and policymakers.

We should say something about our own position. We are both teachers and teacher educators who have spent almost all our working lives in the UK. Our attitudes to education are shaped by the specific contexts in which we have worked and lived, as well as by our ethical and political values, our commitment to social justice. In this book, we are looking at schooling across the world. Education is seen, quite rightly, as a key issue in the Global South. But what type of education? By selling a model of education that is easily deliverable and appears modern (through its use of new technologies) corporate edu-business stands to make huge profits. But there are questions to be asked about how suitable the curriculum is, and about the approaches to learning that are encouraged. Is this a means of liberation, both personal and societal, or a form of educational imperialism?

We are very suspicious of approaches to education that are insufficiently attentive to difference, to local experiences, perspectives and voices. So, being explicit about our own standpoint is important. Most of the specific examples that we cite in this book relate most directly to schools in Anglophone contexts. This doesn't mean that our argument is relevant only to such schools, but there are significant differences in how schooling is done in different cultures and societies.[1]

It is worth noting that what we mean by an Anglophone context is itself not straightforward. In our increasingly interconnected world, English has become the global language. It is estimated that more than 60 per cent of students in non-English-speaking countries study English as a foreign language. In China, English is taught in every school: there are about 350 million students learning English and more teachers of English in China than in the United States. China will thus soon have the largest English-speaking population in the world.[2]

These developments in China are a relatively recent response to changing economic conditions and goals. To understand more about the reasons for the place of English now, in relation to education as well as to the global economy, we need to adopt a historical perspective. Here, as elsewhere in the book, we are suggesting that past debates and decisions can illuminate present circumstances – even if this sometimes means nothing more than understanding how we ended up in the mess we're in.

Adam Unwin and **John Yandell**

1 Robin Alexander, *Culture and Pedagogy* Blackwell, Malden & Oxford, 2000. **2** Qing Liu et al, 'Native-English Speaking Instructors Teaching Writing in China', *Changing English*, 22(1), 2015.

1 What is the point of school?

'Education is the most powerful weapon which you can use to change the world.'

Nelson Mandela

Education is still widely seen as a liberating force – not least by children in poorer countries who are denied access to it. But all too often students experience school as a place that constricts and controls rather than inspires – and that has little relevance to life in the 'real world'. Schools are places where competing interests clash – and where the needs of pupils do not always have priority.

Schools are deeply contradictory places. They offer possibilities of emancipation and development, of learning to become more fully human – and they are places of coercion and belittlement, places where human spirits are crushed. This tension in what schools represent is nothing new. For an optimistic view, here's Sherlock Holmes, looking out of a train window:

Holmes was sunk in profound thought and hardly opened his mouth until we had passed Clapham Junction.

'It's a very cheery thing to come into London by any of these lines which run high and allow you to look down upon the houses like this.'

I thought he was joking, for the view was sordid enough, but he soon explained himself.

'Look at those big, isolated clumps of buildings rising up above the slates, like brick islands in a lead-colored sea.'

'The board-schools.'

'Lighthouses, my boy! Beacons of the future! Capsules with hundreds of bright little seeds in each, out of which will spring the wiser, better England of the future...'[1]

Holmes was looking at the board schools built in London in the aftermath of the 1870 Education Act, the legislation that established a universal right to elementary education in England and Wales. In his view, the well-built, large-windowed, airy three-story Victorian buildings represented an advance – an indication of the state's investment in education and its commitment to the betterment of the working class: a reason to take a bright view of the future.

For a contrary view, here are the words of Barrie, a 19-year-old mineworker, in conversation with his former teacher, reflecting on his experience of schooling in the 1970s:

> I think a teacher's a person that wants to put intelligence into someone like a bloody factory animal. I think the perfect teaching system would be to have kids there with built-in impulses to be sat in rows, take it all in, write it all down and remember it for ever. I mean they're trying to make them like ruddy little computers.[2]

Here, school is experienced as an instrument of repression, of domination and the denial of individuality, of freedom, of agency or motivation.

What are the reasons for these radically different views of schooling? To address this question, we have to consider both the internal operation of school and how schools are situated in the wider society. What kind of system is the school system? What does it do – and how does it do it?

There is also the glaring issue of disparities: how wealth, whether at individual, regional, national or international level, determines a person's educational opportunities; how gender can similarly influence educational chances. These disparities are particularly acute in the Global South, as has been recognized by the Education for All (EFA) movement:

Launched in 1990 by UNESCO, UNDP, UNICEF and the World Bank. Participants endorsed an 'expanded vision of learning' and pledged to universalize primary education and massively reduce illiteracy by the end of the decade.[3]

Ten years later these goals were far from being achieved. The World Education Forum in Dakar, Senegal, in 2000 reaffirmed its commitment to achieving Education for All by the year 2015. UNESCO was to lead this with a focus on six key education goals, including comprehensive and free primary education for all, eliminating gender disparities and a focus on numeracy and literacy. In 2014 the UNESCO global monitoring reports pointed to some progress; yet in sub-Saharan Africa there are still 30 million children out of school. There is no doubt about the challenges, the inequalities and the lack of entitlement that continue to be the experience of many in the Global South. These are real, material disparities – and they matter. But access to education is only one aspect of what is at stake. Always and everywhere, it is necessary to ask about the purposes of education: whose interests are being served?

What, then, is the contribution that school can make? It has long been assumed that improving educational outcomes is all about schooling, and this, as we can see from the EFA agenda (above), is represented as a question of mass access. But we might want to ask: universal provision of what? What actually happens in schools and classrooms? Whose knowledge is it anyway?

These questions will recur throughout the book. Here, though, to illustrate something of the complexity of the issues involved, let's look at a key moment in the history of schooling as a global phenomenon. It is a moment that reveals education as a battleground, fought over by very powerful vested interests. And it is a moment with far-reaching consequences: its effects are still evident today.

The language of imperialism

Back in the 1830s, when the British Empire was reaching into every corner of the world, a debate was raging between the civil servants and the missionaries. The argument was about what an appropriate education system would look like in the Indian subcontinent. The missionaries were in favor of using the indigenous learned languages of Arabic and Sanskrit, the languages into which they were already translating the Bible, as the medium of instruction and indoctrination. This approach, they believed, would be one that would most readily enable them to win hearts and minds (and converts).

The civil servants had other ideas. They favored the use of English, arguing that money should be diverted away from existing Arabic- and Sanskrit-medium schools and put towards the development of an English-medium education system.[4] One of the civil servants, Thomas Babington Macaulay, made the case in a trenchantly expressed 'Minute on Indian Education'.[5]

I have conversed both here and at home with men distinguished by their proficiency in the Eastern tongues... I have never found one among them who could deny that a single shelf of a good European library was worth the whole native literature of India and Arabia...

The claims of our own language it is hardly necessary to recapitulate. It stands pre-eminent even among the languages of the West. It abounds with works of imagination not inferior to the noblest which Greece has bequeathed to us, – with models of every species of eloquence, – with historical composition, which, considered merely as narratives, have seldom been surpassed, and which, considered as vehicles of ethical and political instruction, have never been equalled – with just and lively representations of human life and human nature, – with the most profound speculations on metaphysics, morals, government, jurisprudence, trade, – with full and correct information respecting every experimental science which tends to preserve the health, to increase the comfort, or to expand the intellect of man. Whoever knows that language has ready access to all the vast intellectual wealth which all the wisest nations of the earth have created and hoarded in the course of ninety generations. It may safely be said that the literature now extant in that language is of greater value than all the literature which three hundred years ago was extant in all the languages of the world together.

Even from this historical distance, the claims that Macaulay makes on behalf of English language and literature are breathtaking. The superiority of English language and culture over all others is both taken for granted and enacted in the argument. Here, at a moment that is close to the beginning of European nation states' involvement and investment in schooling, education is not just implicated in the history of British imperialism, it is integral to the imperialist project. Here, too, it is pretty clear that what knowledge is valuable depends on one's point of view – and how much power one has to enforce this view on others.

Macaulay's arguments prevailed. English became the medium of instruction, not only in schools in the subcontinent but across the Empire, thereby helping to construct an indigenous cadre, loyal to the imperial center, whose efforts would ensure the efficient operation of a global bureaucracy, as vital to the business of government as to commerce itself. This, of course, was what was at stake, and perhaps rather more important than Macaulay's overt emphasis on the civilizing virtues of English.

Also in the 1830s, the British state established a national school system in Ireland. As with British policy in India, this was not intended to emancipate but to control. A series of textbooks, or 'readers', was published, initially for use in Ireland. Over the following 30 years or so, the same readers were to be found in schools in Canada, in England, and across the Empire.

These readers provided the basis for a centralized, homogeneous curriculum – one that paid no attention whatsoever to local circumstances, cultures or histories and promoted 'a view of the world that placed Britain, Christianity and the English language at the normative centre'.[6] The textbooks, like the schools in which they were used, were instruments of imperial domination. And they might reasonably be regarded as having contributed to the contemporary position of English as a global language.

Things have moved on, of course. The fact that there are 350 million students of English in Chinese schools is only distantly related to the history of British (or American) imperialism. But it would be a mistake to imagine that, in this postcolonial era, schooling is always and everywhere designed to further the interests – material, intellectual or spiritual – of the learners.

Postcolonial schooling: the 'Diploma Disease' era

The term 'diploma disease' was coined in 1976 by Ronald Dore as the title of what is now seen as a seminal book.[7] Dore was a sociologist with a long-term interest in how countries that are part of what we now would refer to as the Global South approached economic development. The particular focus of his 20-year research was on the role of education and qualifications in this development. Dore used an example to explain the spread of the disease:

A bus company may 'normally' require a junior secondary leaving certificate for bus conductors and a senior secondary leaving certificate for the slightly better paid clerks. But as the number of senior certificate holders grows far larger than the number of clerkships that are available, some of them decide that £5 a week as a bus conductor is better than nothing at all. The bus company gives them preference. Soon all the available conductor slots are filled by senior certificate holders: a senior certificate has become a necessary qualification for the job.[8]

Rethinking education

This is sometimes called qualification inflation, where increasingly one needs higher qualifications for entry to certain jobs – not because of the skills required to do the job but because the qualification starts to function as a filtering mechanism. Dore was interested in how this featured in and influenced the labor markets of these 'modernizing' economies. Dore's work challenges the notion that there is a simple, rational and socially progressive causal relation between apparent improvements in the level of schooling and economic benefits. There is, though, another aspect of his work that is interesting, which is how this qualification inflation affects the educational experience itself – what it means for the learners. One might expect that the need for higher qualifications would lead to schooling being seen as more important and thus improve the quality of both provision and participation in educational processes. If it had this effect then, as Dore argued, education would produce better people – more responsible citizens, more civilized, thoughtful and appreciative human beings, with a better quality of life.

But this is not what happened. Schools and students became obsessed with getting the qualifications. Learning for its own sake (the intrinsically worthwhile pursuit of knowledge and understanding) or even learning for more utilitarian purposes (to acquire the skills necessary to do a particular job) started to become irrelevant. The only learning that counted was learning to pass examinations. Dore's diagnosis is sharply worded – and as apt today as when he produced it:

> ...more qualification earning is *mere* qualification earning – ritualistic, tedious, suffused with anxiety and boredom, destructive of curiosity and imagination, in short, anti-educational.[9]

Dore's description captures an enduring and increasingly global phenomenon. As will become clear in later chapters, the 'diploma disease' is now virulent, particularly in the form of the 'high stakes' assessment regimes that exert such a pernicious, debilitating influence on education. The outcomes of assessment – tests and examinations – are increasingly important for all participants: for students, whose future careers, in terms of entry into further study or into the labor market, are determined not by what they can accomplish but rather by the mark they have been awarded; and for their teachers, who themselves are judged not by the role they have played in the development of other human beings but rather by the test scores that their students attain. The problem identified by Dore, caused in part by qualification inflation, now appears as the strategic goal of many educational systems – where schools take on an exam factory role rather than contributing to the wider education and development of the population.[10]

Cartoon by John De Rosier / Times Union, reprinted with permission

We tend to think of education as a good thing in itself, and as a means of empowerment or liberation. We are inclined to see schools as Sherlock Holmes saw them, as lighthouses or beacons, not as factories or prison-houses. Sometimes, though, they are both.

Learning in and out of school

People's educational experiences vary considerably. Your own experiences at school, positive and negative, will affect your attitudes to the claims that are made about education. Your knowledge, understanding and previous experience are not, of course, confined to what you learned in formal schooling. Your learning will have taken many guises. Learning happens from birth onwards (and very possibly even before that, in the womb). The moment a child is born, they enter a richly educative environment. Their learning is, from the very beginning, socially and culturally mediated: they make sense of the things around them in interaction with other human beings, mainly their caregivers and other family members. These processes do not stop when more formal education starts. Family, peers, community members and work colleagues continue to play a vitally important role in learning and development throughout one's life.

Throughout this book there are 'cases' – examples to help explain, illustrate and analyze different educational issues and phenomena. These are mainly concerned with what we would call formal education (that is, within schools) but it is important to recognize that these cases will always be located within wider contexts. Those contexts will have many differences and will exert profound, shaping influences on the educational process. So, for example, what can be accomplished within a school is subject to the constraints of the material conditions of existence experienced by the children and young people who attend it: poverty, cramped and insanitary housing, disease and inadequate diet all impair the capacity of human beings to learn.

No educational process is context-free; no school exists in a vacuum. And all schools operate within contexts that are both material and ideological, shaped not only by the availability of physical resources but also by the interests, values and purposes of those who are in a position to influence the work that schools do. We can see this in the two cases looked at earlier. The decision to educate the colonies in English was in the context of British imperialism. The diploma disease was in the context of an increasingly competitive labor market in developing economies.

Such contexts, however, like the processes of schooling themselves, are never stable, never simple. They are affected by changes in society, by political beliefs and ideologies, by economic factors, by developments in science and technology, as well as by changes in education policy and practice. And schools remain sites of struggle, places where competing interests clash. English, like other European languages, may have been introduced into schools in other areas of the globe as part of an imperialist project; but it has been appropriated by others, refashioned as a language of resistance and emancipation. Even within the exam factory, possibilities remain for education to be differently imagined, engaged in for quite different purposes.

Is technology the answer?

Of all the many ways in which the complexities of schooling can be – and have been – reduced to simple statements of cause and effect, currently the most popular is the view that technology trumps everything. Janus-like, this view faces in opposite directions simultaneously.

For the techno-pessimists, the rise of the new digital technologies spells the end of civilization as we know it – and the blighting of all that is of educational value.

The young, addicted to the easy pleasures of video gaming and the immediate gratification provided by a life lived online, have not the time, nor the inclination, nor indeed the attention span, to engage in the activities that would enable them to develop intellectually: sustained study, reading and academic rigor are all beyond them. Why should the 'digital natives' learn to mull things over, to ruminate, to analyze, when the forms of contemporary communication so powerfully enforce the expectation of immediacy? 'Like' – and move on.

For the techno-optimists, the same phenomenon signals the obsolescence of traditional schooling. Why should anyone bother with the laborious acquisition of knowledge when we have almost infinite stores of information at our fingertips? The young are growing up in a world where they are almost constantly (digitally) connected to their families, their friends, wider interest groups and to the internet. They can rapidly and continuously share ideas, recount experiences, raise problems, voice opinions, get feedback and so on. Smartphone ownership is almost ubiquitous in the Global North and increasingly available in the Global South. Society is digitally connected – so why go to school? And what is the point of employing teachers when technology provides cheaper and more reliable access to education?

Both these versions of technological determinism should be rejected. Some of the claims that are made on behalf of the new digital technologies deserve to be treated with skepticism. In part, this is because one always needs to ask about the uses to which new technologies are put – about whose interests they are serving. But it is also because of how earlier technological transformations played out. The Gutenberg revolution, for example, did not mean that print superseded earlier forms of communication and representation, any more than the spread of mass literacy meant that people stopped talking to each other. Each new development tends to sit alongside and interact in complicated ways with existing technologies, not to replace them.

Smartphones and the connectivity they bring with them offer powerful resources for learning. But we need to attend carefully to how they are used, and how these uses change over time and from place to place. Students can – and often do – have (digital) conversations with each other about school work beyond the school day. This can be positive: teachers are already exploiting some of this potential, planning for different kinds of collaborative, dialogic learning. On the other hand, conflicts between students that start in school continue outside school, as they always have, but this can now happen in a more sustained and damaging fashion: cyber-bullying is not to be taken lightly.

Educators clearly need to engage with the new digital landscape. It is odd that some schools seek to ban students from any use of smartphones on the school premises – as if there were something inherently malign about the technology. It is even stranger that recent shifts in education policy, particularly in Britain, amount to an outright refusal to engage with the fact that there has been a transformation in the modes of communication and representation.

Beyond the school gates, people (and especially young people) are adept at working with the resources that the new digital technologies have made available. In their everyday lives, they work on screen, writing and designing, combining still and moving images and sounds as well as words. In school, on the other hand, a much more limited version of literacy remains dominant – a version that would largely have been familiar to Macaulay in the 19th century. And this form of the digital divide – this separation of school knowledge from out-of-school practices – certainly does not serve the interests of the learners who are thus forced to inhabit two quite separate worlds.

1 A Conan Doyle, *The Adventure of the Naval Treaty*, 1893. **2** Peter Medway, *Finding a Language*, Writers and Readers Cooperative, London, 1980, p 30. **3** UNESCO, nin.tl/EFAgoals **4** AS Canagarajah, *Resisting Linguistic Imperialism in English Teaching*, Oxford University Press, Oxford, 1999. **5** nin.tl/Macaulaystudy **6** Patrick Walsh, 'English in the history of imperialism: teaching the empire how to read', in V Ellis et al (eds), *Rethinking English in Schools: towards a new and constructive stage*, Continuum, London & New York, 2007. **7** Ronald Dore, *The Diploma Disease: Education, Qualification and Development*, George Allen & Unwin, London, 1976. **8** Ibid, p 5. **9** Ibid, p ix. **10** Merryn Hutchings, *Exam factories? The impact of accountability measures on children and young people*. NUT, London, 2015, nin.tl/examfactories

2 How we learn – in and out of school

'The only thing that interferes with my learning is my education.'

Albert Einstein

Government ministers often talk about education as if it were a production line, with knowledge transferred from teachers to students in measurable chunks. Schools and teachers are judged by output in terms of exam results and league-table performance. Yet the way we learn as babies or as workers could not be more different. The best educational experiences are those that break out of the exam-factory model.

Teacher: 'What do you go to school for?'
Pupil: 'To learn.'
Teacher: 'So stop messing about with Jamal and get on with what you're meant to be doing.'

You have probably witnessed – or even participated in – a conversation similar to the one between the teacher and pupil above. It is a familiar exchange in classrooms across the world. Embedded in it are two assumptions that are so widespread, so taken for granted, that they pass unnoticed. The first is that learning happens in schools (and, by implication, not elsewhere); the second is that learning happens in individuals (and so interaction between pupils is construed as 'off-task behavior', a distraction from the serious business of learning).

These assumptions are part of what might be seen as a common-sense view of education. In this model, learning is a process of transmission. The teacher is the one who is already knowledgeable, whose role is to transmit knowledge to the pupil, the one who is not-yet-knowledgeable. The teacher, or the teacher's teacher, determines in advance what is worth knowing; the pupil is the (sometimes) grateful beneficiary of this knowledge. In this process of knowledge transmission, the teacher is assisted by artefacts that have usually been specifically designed for educational purposes including textbooks, worksheets, displays and so on.

For much of the history of formal education, this model of learning has been massively influential, informing the day-to-day practice of teachers and their pupils. The following scenario is probably already familiar to you.

The traditional history lesson

Students are seated in rows of desks facing the front. The teacher is positioned at the front; he has a desk and a board for presentation purposes. The class are 11-year-olds studying a period of history from 200 years ago in their country. The teacher introduces today's topic, explaining how it follows on from the last lesson. He hands back marked tests from the last lesson. He indicates that all marks of 8/10 or better are good ('Well done!'); anything less means that the pupils need to work harder and revise more. The teacher then dictates (using his own notes), while students write the teacher's words in an exercise book. If any student talks to another pupil, they are reprimanded. After 15 minutes, the teacher stops dictating and explains/expands on the historical context; he asks if everybody understands. There is only one question: someone asks how to spell the word 'government'.

The teacher then hands out the class textbook. He tells students to turn to page 42 and copy out a section that summarizes a specific Act of Parliament that has been referred to earlier. They are given 10 minutes to do this. Some students are quicker than others at this copying. The teacher then uses the board to present a series of dates of significant events. Students copy these down from the board; this takes 10 minutes. They are then asked to spend 10 minutes reading and revising their notes from the last lesson and this lesson. They put their exercise books away and are handed a test paper with a series of questions. They have 10 minutes to do this. These questions prompt the students to recall which events happened on certain dates, who was in power at the time and so on. They hand their answers in to the teacher. He explains that next week they will be moving on to the next 15 years in this period, where there was a change of government. The lesson ends and the students depart.

In this scenario, learning would appear to be a matter of acquiring and memorizing certain pieces of information. The pupils demonstrate that they have accomplished that learning by regurgitating the appropriate bit of information in response to a set of prompt questions. Equally, the failure to reproduce the correct answer is an indication that learning has *not* happened. In such cases, there is the clear implication that the responsibility for this failure lies with the pupil. The lesson has been properly taught, or delivered, even if it has not been properly learnt, or received.

Most learning, in most situations in everyday life, does not look anything like this – and this is one of the things that make schools such peculiar places.

Take the learning that almost all human beings achieve in the first few years of our lives, before we go anywhere near a school. We learn at least one language; we learn about other people and about ourselves; we learn a vast amount about the world around us – about how things work and how we can have an effect on what happens. We manage all of this without, in most cases, any formal program of instruction. In other words, we seem to be pretty good at learning (some things, at any rate) without being taught.

As we have understood more about what happens in the first months and years of a child's life, this phase of learning has come to appear even more remarkable. The child's increasing ability to use signs and symbols – gestures, expressions and other meaning-making resources – before, and then alongside, language is a hugely impressive aspect of this learning. But it is more than that: this power of symbolization is the key that transforms everything, that enables the development of thought.

How this power is acquired is fascinating in itself, but also hugely significant in relation to our understanding of learning in other contexts and at later stages of life. Even as very young children, we don't acquire language, or use gesture, simply to get what we want in the world – to satisfy our hunger, or our desire for a toy that is out of reach. As recent work in developmental psychology has emphasized, our capacity to use words and other signs is inseparable from our relationships with other human beings. *Humans are irreducibly social animals.* From the start of our lives, we acquire language because of the strength of our emotional bond with other humans and hence our need to communicate with them. That is why our caregivers don't need to sit us down and give us language lessons. We take the initiative. And from an equally early age, signs enable us to understand not just more about the world but more about how other people see the world. We learn to participate in culturally mediated perspectives on the world because other people matter to us. And sharing in these perspectives is what enables us to learn – to transform our understanding of the world, of others and of ourselves.[1]

Much of the learning that is accomplished in later life bears a much closer resemblance to the learning that we do as young children than it does to the schooling represented in the History lesson described above. Beyond school, learning tends to happen without much obvious or explicit formal instruction. In workplaces and community settings, as well as in the home, people learn by participating in shared activities – and by engaging in dialogue with each other.

The experienced Mayan midwives described in the

The apprenticeship of Mayan midwives

Two sociologists, Jean Lave and Etienne Wenger, became interested in how learning was organized in a range of contexts outside the domain of formal schooling.[2] They looked at how girls and women become midwives within the Mayan community in the Yucatan region of Mexico. What they observed was a type of apprenticeship learning.

The midwives provide a service within their community. They are expert at techniques of birthing including dealing with complications such as breech birth. They also understand how to use the herbal medicines, massage and ritual procedures that are part of the birth process in their community.

How does learning occur to achieve this skilled and important role within the community? It does not involve schooling, classes or formal instruction. The apprentice midwives are almost always the daughters of experienced midwives. The process of learning happens over many years. This starts as young children where they are exposed to the day-to-day practices and specific knowledge the role requires.

For example, she could be sitting in the corner when an expectant mother visits for a prenatal massage. As she gets older she might start to help with some of the basic practicalities, such as mixing massage oils. She would hear accounts of difficult cases and what approaches were used. As she becomes a teenager she might attend postnatal visits with her mother/grandmother. Perhaps after having a child herself, she might attend births and assist. She might start giving massages to selected clients. At some point she might decide she wants to do this as a job (not all daughters of midwives will become midwives). Then her role develops, she will gradually take over aspects of the role, starting with the routine and tedious parts and moving on to the more complicated parts. Eventually she will be capable of all aspects of the midwife role on her own. In due course she might have younger members of her family assisting with more menial tasks. So the cycle of apprenticeship learning continues.

box have more knowledge, more expertise, than the novices – just as caregivers know more and can do more than their young children. But their knowledge and skills are not transmitted in a series of lessons. Instead, learning happens through participation in situated practice. This represents, therefore, a different model of learning from the one that has traditionally

Rethinking education

been associated with schooling. Some would argue that there are good reasons for these different models of learning, and that these reasons relate to the different kinds of knowledge that are being acquired in these different contexts. According to this view, the particular kind of knowledge that schools have to offer demands a particular kind of learning, and hence a particular way of organizing the learning and the learners.

Subsequent chapters will come back to this claim when they look at knowledge and the curriculum. But the point here is that there is a fundamental problem with the transmission model: it doesn't seem to work very well as a means of enabling learning. This is not a fresh discovery. More than 80 years ago, Lev Vygotsky, the Russian psychologist, observed the following:

> Experience demonstrates that direct instruction in concepts is impossible. It is pedagogically fruitless. The teacher who attempts to use this approach achieves nothing but a mindless learning of words, an empty verbalism that simulates or imitates the presence of concepts in the child. Under these conditions, the child learns not the concept but the word, and this word is taken over by the child through memory rather than thought. Such knowledge turns out to be inadequate in any meaningful application. This mode of instruction... substitutes the learning of dead and empty verbal schemes for the mastery of living knowledge.[3]

The rote learning that Vygotsky describes – the memorizing of gobbets of information without any sense of what these gobbets might mean, why they might be interesting or important – is what Charles Dickens attacked through the figure of Thomas Gradgrind in his novel *Hard Times* (see box overleaf). It is an approach which in recent years has become increasingly fashionable.

Vygotsky's scathing criticism of this model of learning needs to be taken seriously. His argument is that real learning – learning that is worth the name, and worth spending time on – involves the development of thought. Without this, all one is left with is 'empty verbalism' – the training of bright parrots, not of human minds. Think back to the History lesson described at the

---

The Gradgrind model of education

Charles Dickens' 1854 novel, Hard Times, *includes the character of Thomas Gradgrind, a teacher whose practice is defined by narrow, soulless utilitarianism. Here we see him at work.*

Thomas Gradgrind, sir. A man of realities. A man of fact and calculations. A man who proceeds upon the principle that two and two are four, and nothing over, and who is not to be talked into allowing for anything over. Thomas Gradgrind, sir – peremptorily Thomas – Thomas Gradgrind. With a rule and a pair of scales, and the multiplication table always in his pocket, sir, ready to weigh and measure any parcel of human nature, and tell you exactly what it comes to. It is a mere question of figures, a case of simple arithmetic...

'Girl number twenty,' said Mr Gradgrind, squarely pointing with his square forefinger, 'I don't know that girl. Who is that girl?'

'Sissy Jupe, sir,' explained number twenty, blushing, standing up, and curtseying.

'Sissy is not a name,' said Mr Gradgrind. 'Don't call yourself Sissy. Call yourself Cecilia.'

'My father as calls me Sissy, sir,' returned the young girl in a trembling voice, and with another curtsey.

'Then he has no business to do it,' said Mr Gradgrind. 'Tell him he mustn't. Cecilia Jupe. Let me see. What is your father?'

'He belongs to the horse-riding, if you please, sir.'

... 'Very well, then. He is a veterinary surgeon, a farrier and horsebreaker. Give me your definition of a horse.'

(Sissy Jupe thrown into the greatest alarm by this demand.)

'Girl number twenty unable to define a horse!' said Mr Gradgrind, for the general behoof of all the little pitchers. 'Girl number twenty possessed of no facts, in reference to one of the commonest of animals! Some boy's definition of a horse. Bitzer, yours.'

... 'Quadruped. Graminivorous. Forty teeth, namely twenty-four grinders, four eye-teeth, and twelve incisive. Sheds coat in the spring; in marshy countries, sheds hoofs, too. Hoofs hard, but requiring to be shod with iron. Age known by marks in mouth.' Thus (and much more) Bitzer.

'Now girl number twenty,' said Mr Gradgrind. 'You know what a horse is.'

---

start of this chapter. The learning that is taking place here is, to a very large extent, the learning of facts – of names, dates, events – facts dictated by the teacher and memorized by the learner. There is no opportunity here for the learners to consider different interpretations, to weigh up the evidence, to consult different sources, to ask questions and to develop hypotheses. There is, in short, no opportunity for the students to act as historians or to learn about the practice of history: their role is to absorb information. And there is certainly no opportunity for the students to make connections between what they are studying and anything else in their own lives and experiences.

One of the great attractions of the Gradgrind model is its simplicity. It is an input-output model, where what is learnt is the same as what is taught. This makes it very easy to plan (since the lesson that is taught is precisely the same as the lesson that the teacher had envisaged before the lesson began), very easy to replicate (since the same lesson, using the same materials, could readily be taught in thousands of different classrooms), and very easy to assess (since what is to be learnt has been specified in advance and consists of isolable facts, so there are straightforward, right or wrong answers). To call this a model of learning would be misleading. The reason that the Gradgrind model is so simple is that it ignores the questions of how and why learning might happen: it assumes that pupils are, in effect, blank slates or empty containers, passive recipients of the knowledge that schooling provides.

This is what makes the Gradgrind approach an attractive model for politicians and policymakers. If learning is so straightforward, education becomes simply a matter of making sure that the right things are getting taught (transmitted) and that the teachers are teaching (transmitting) what they are told to. A huge proportion of education policy over the past few decades would appear to have started from these assumptions. Some of the people who work within educational settings have encouraged the view that learning is a very straightforward affair, that it is reducible to single processes of input and output, cause and effect; and there have been others who proclaim that neuroscience has all the answers – that all we need to do is to peer inside the brain and there we'll see how learning happens.

These ideas are reductive, largely mistaken and massively unhelpful. They get in the way of effective, meaningful education because they are based on an inadequate model of learning. Such approaches fail to take account of the interests of the learners. They also do not understand what real learning looks like: it is social and dialogic, situated and contingent, often messy and unpredictable. These are the characteristics of the learning that almost all human beings accomplish in the first years of our lives – and what we learn in this period is pretty impressive. But these are also the characteristics of learning more generally – and it is bad education policy to ignore them.

Street and school mathematics

As evidence that traditional classroom models are problematic, consider the findings of a team of researchers who investigated the mathematical skills and understanding of two groups of people in Brazil.[4]

The first were boys and young men who worked on market stalls in the favelas, and had had some experience of schooling. When they were at work, they showed that they were perfectly capable of coping with arithmetic calculations to do with price and quantity: with unwavering consistency, they got the answers right. Placed in a classroom and confronted with equivalent calculations in the form of pencil and paper tests, they were hopelessly inaccurate, making errors that might have seemed to reveal a lack of understanding of the mathematical concepts and procedures with which they were dealing.

Rethinking education

The second group were farmers and agricultural workers. They, too, demonstrated the capacity to carry out quite sophisticated calculations of the area of irregularly shaped fields, and to work out the quantities of seed crops they would need to plant these fields. And, like the market-stall workers, they struggled when they were confronted with the same mathematical problems in the form in which they had encountered them at school, as paper exercises.

How could the same people be both good and bad at mathematics? The common-sense assumption is that someone either can or cannot perform particular arithmetic operations, and that setting them a test is a perfectly accurate way of finding out what they can and cannot do. The same assumption underpins all the statements that are made about the percentage of school-leavers, or of the general population, who are 'illiterate' – as if measuring literacy were equally straightforward.

What happened when the participants in this research were asked to do the school version of mathematics was that they tried to apply a series of half-remembered 'rules' – ways of dealing with numbers and with arith-metical operations that they had been taught in school, but which had possibly never really made sense to them. So they misapplied the rules, and got the answers wrong. But when they were posed the same problem in a context that did make sense to them – where the math was meaningful – they showed that they had a perfectly adequate understanding of the mathematical concepts and operations involved. Their learning, in other words, was situated in the real world, contingent on the everyday experience of their working lives, within which, of course, they had a powerful motive to get the sums right – their interests were very much at stake.

So, if this is what learning looks like, what are the implications for what happens in school? If learning involves the interests of learners, mobilized in particular circumstances, what is involved in teaching?

Teaching and pedagogy

The word 'pedagogy' tends to be used about formal teaching situations – so it is more often encountered in contexts like classrooms than in relation to apprenticeship learning like that of the Yucatan midwives. Pedagogy can refer to the theory and practice of education – the knowledge that is involved in the formation of teachers. But the word 'pedagogy' is also more widely used to refer to any conscious attempt by one person to intervene in another person's learning. In practice, pedagogy is inseparable from the particular contexts and social relations in which it takes place.

How classrooms are organized makes a huge difference to the learning that is accomplished. Approaches to teaching are shaped by a wide range

---

The complexity of classrooms[5]

Context variables

Teacher characteristics
Gender, age, experience, social class, training, personality, ideology

Student characteristics
Age, health, values, personality, social class, gender, cultural background, interests, friendships, previous experiences, attitudes to learning

Class characteristics
Size, social class, age range, cultural mix

Classroom environment
Space, layout, resources

Subject characteristics
Subject matter, level of complexity, links with general interest

School characteristics
Size, buildings, facilities, ethos, disciplinary policy, admissions system, intake, reputation

National and community characteristics
Political regime, socio-economic position, population density, location

Characteristics of the occasion
Time of the day/week, preceding lesson, weather, time of year

---

Rethinking education

of factors, both material (such as space, class size and available resources) and ideological or theoretical. Pedagogic approaches might be prescribed at various levels within the education system, but it is in the classroom, in the interactions of particular teachers and learners, that they are realized.

To start to understand how complicated, dynamic and unpredictable classrooms are, take a look at the 'variables framework' in the box below. This framework could be applied to most educational situations where there are schools, teachers and students. To introduce the notion of 'variability' is to acknowledge that what happens within classrooms is by no means standard, and that it is influenced by all kinds of different factors. This includes the diversity of individuals, their varied ways of working

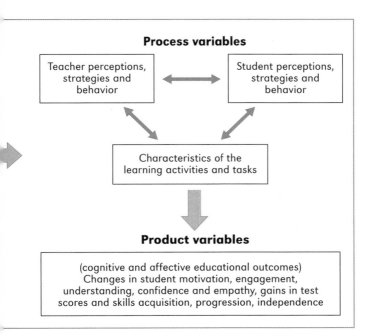

Process variables

Teacher perceptions, strategies and behavior ⟷ Student perceptions, strategies and behavior

Characteristics of the learning activities and tasks

Product variables

(cognitive and affective educational outcomes) Changes in student motivation, engagement, understanding, confidence and empathy, gains in test scores and skills acquisition, progression, independence

How we learn – in and out of school

and studying as well as different institutional practices. You can probably think back to your own educational experiences and recognize many of the variables at play and how they helped or hindered your learning.

With the 'History lesson' described earlier, one can clearly see what is happening with the 'process variables' (the teacher is dictating, the students are writing and so forth). But it appears in this lesson that this is being done with almost no consideration of the 'context variables'. Any effective teaching needs to start by understanding the context – and, in particular, understanding the students. What are these students interested in? Are there aspects of their culture and background that might relate to the subject? What previous understanding of the topic might they have? How do individuals and small groups behave? What friendships exist? Who might work well together, and where might there be conflicts, clashes, disagreements? These are just some of the factors about students that a teacher might want to take into account when planning.

But there are other context variables, too. For example: how much space is there in the classroom? How flexible are seating and tables? Does the disposition of the furniture allow for small group work? What resources are available? What time of day is it? Will the students arrive at the lesson feeling hungry or tired, excited or subdued? A teacher who is 'contextually aware' will be in a better position to come up with approaches that are effective and appropriate, for example by introducing activities that engage and interest students, and materials that relate to their lives.

The framework also includes 'product variables'. Policymakers and politicians as well as the media often focus on 'products' of the educational system. Have exam results improved? What facts have students actually learnt? How does this align with labor-market needs? All too often they rely on league tables to compare school outcomes, making implicit and unexamined assumptions about what constitutes successful learning. But the framework recognizes that learning is more complicated – that there are other kinds of product. Learning happens over time and often what is learned is not measured or measurable. Students might develop their confidence, their independence, understand how to work with others and find things out. These are essential life skills that are not measurable by an exam or test run at a particular time in the learning cycle.

Cultures in contact

As a positive example of teaching and learning, let's look in detail at a joint project in the UK between a large city museum and a number of schools called 'cultures in contact'. This had the overarching aim of improving the students' understanding of what happens when different cultures interact through processes such as trade, imperialism and globalization.

The project ran over three years, starting when students were about 12 years old. Each year, students took part in a 'museum sandwich': an activity at school; a day at the museum; followed by a 'plenary' activity back in school, where students had the opportunity to reflect together on what they had experienced. The focus in the middle year of the project was on West Africa during the period of European imperialism. It involved teaching staff from schools as well as museum enactors (people acting out historical roles). Throughout the sessions there was substantial use of supporting resources such as role cards, information sheets, pictures, maps, artefacts and so on, all of which had been designed to be accessible to and appropriate for 13-year-olds.

In school: West Africa trading game (pre-colonization)

This was in a typical classroom setting with approximately 30 students for 90 minutes. There was an initial briefing, which set the scene of what was happening in Benin (West Africa) at this time. This included the use of museum artefacts from the era. The main part of the session was a mix of role-play and simulation. Students worked in groups of five or six that represented different villages. They made various products (see the diagram showing product shapes[6]) which they 'traded' to earn wealth for their village. They did this by interacting with each other, with other villages and with the merchant prince (played by a museum enactor) who was a powerful figure with wealth and connections.

Some villages were richer than others, possessing more or fewer natural resources (represented by paper) and technology (represented by scissors, pencils and rulers). The game was very active: students needed to make decisions about what to produce and how to do so, what resources they needed, how much they could afford to pay or how they could bargain, what deals they might make with other villages or the merchant prince and so on. The prices of the products changed during the game, reflecting overall production (supply) and the demand by the European agent (who was located at a port). The villages could see their relative wealth and feel the unfairness of some of the trading relationships. The simulation activity was followed by a debriefing session. Students were asked about their feelings, how they interpreted different aspects of the game, and how this related to historical context.

Trade items

Resources, materials and products supplied by villages

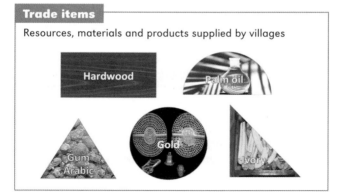

Hardwood

Palm oil

Gum Arabic

Gold

Ivory

In the museum: 'scramble for Africa'

This occupied around 150 students for a whole day. In the morning session students were split into groups of 15. The groups took part in a gallery carousel, hearing stories from museum enactors and taking part in activities – such as identifying 'traded' objects and the stories behind these within the Africa gallery.

In the afternoon they were organized into three groups of 50 students who worked in large spaces in the museum education center. Each group was split into seven European country teams (Britain, France, Belgium, Germany, Portugal, Spain, Italy – the countries present at the Berlin Conference of 1884-85). They worked in their country teams, familiarizing themselves with their country's situation, motives and interests in Africa. They had maps of Africa (with various European settlements and sources of raw materials shown) and information sheets to help them.

The information for the Britain group included, for example:

- 'Britain has the largest Empire in 1880 and does not want to have its position challenged by other European countries.
- 'Britain needs to keep its trade routes to India via the Cape and the Suez Canal safe at all costs.
- 'Britain wants to ensure that it has access to raw materials for industrial production, such as palm oil from West Africa.
- 'Britain needs to maintain the areas it has been using to trade and gain new ones to ensure that British manufacturers have markets for their products, including textiles, hardware and firearms.'

In their country groups, students decided on what they wanted and the negotiation strategies they might use. The country team then divided and moved to seven 'Berlin conference' tables where there was a representative from each of the other six countries. Within this group they argued, debated and negotiated with the aim of achieving a partition of Africa. The final 'agreement' used a blank map, annotated to illustrate the way in which they had carved up the continent.

The session then moved to whole group work with a facilitator leading a presentation of what actually happened at the

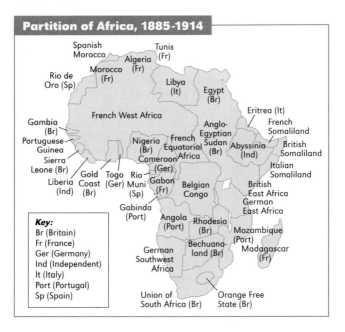

Partition of Africa, 1885-1914

Spanish Morocco
Tunis (Fr)
Algeria (Fr)
Morocco (Fr)
Rio de Oro (Sp)
Libya (It)
Egypt (Br)
Eritrea (It)
French West Africa
French Somaliland
Gambia (Br)
Anglo-Egyptian Sudan (Br)
Portuguese Guinea
Nigeria (Br)
French Equatorial Africa
Abyssinia (Ind)
British Somaliland
Sierra Leone (Br)
Cameroon (Ger)
Italian Somaliland
Liberia (Ind)
Gold Coast (Br)
Togo (Ger)
Rio Muni (Sp)
Gabon (Fr)
Belgian Congo
British East Africa
German East Africa
Gabinda (Port)
Angola (Port)
Rhodesia (Br)
Mozambique (Port)
German Southwest Africa
Bechuana-land (Br)
Madagascar (Fr)
Union of South Africa (Br)
Orange Free State (Br)

Key:
Br (Britain)
Fr (France)
Ger (Germany)
Ind (Independent)
It (Italy)
Port (Portugal)
Sp (Spain)

Berlin Conference in 1885. A key resource for this was the partition of Africa map (see above). Students could compare this with their 'agreements'. They were also asked who was missing from the conference, with follow-up questions about the implications of there being no participation by any Africans – people who might have views on decisions about borders and about the idea that their land was 'owned' by European people and governments of which they know nothing.

In school: role-plays from colonial life

The final part of the sandwich was enacted in school. The story was that students were back in their villages in West Africa. Colonial rule had begun and was emphasized by a facilitator, in role as a British colonial officer (signified by accent, air of authority and a pith helmet) dramatically making the announcement that the British had just taken over the country, that the African people were now the subjects of a white queen, and that the new governor was on his way.

Within their villages, students took on roles such as trader, healer, farmer, warrior or chief. Each village needed to consider how it would react to British rule. Would villagers co-operate, leave the area, or resist? What would be the best course of action in the long term? They had village meetings to discuss their personal and village predicaments and were asked to plan a freeze-frame where they acted out a difficult scenario. Each village took its turn to present its 'freeze-frame' and the whole group then became involved in analyzing what was going on. Each village explained and summarized its feelings about colonial rule. The facilitator de-briefed, highlighting the diversity of responses and reactions. A plenary recapped on the various elements and made linkages between three separate 'cultures in contact' elements: pre-colonial trading, the scramble for Africa and life in the empire.

Why the 'cultures in contact' model is so rich

This case study has been studied in such detail because it involves more than one 'traditional' lesson. It includes a typical classroom setting but also the use of external community resources (the museum). Thinking of the the variables framework introduced earlier, it is clear that the approaches used with students here are taking account of a host of factors that are not considered in more traditional lessons.

Consider some of the context variables that might be important. Who were these students? In this case they were from inner-city London state schools with diverse intakes in terms of cultural and ethnic backgrounds. How might the students have been interested in these topics? What did they already know, for example, about related aspects of geography, history and economics? Some of that information would come from their formal school curriculum; but what about other less obvious influences on their previous knowledge and experiences?

Certainly some of the students were from African heritage backgrounds, and there would have been multiple reasons why they lived in the UK. Some of these may well have been linked to imperialism and trade (including the slave trade). Then there were children from other refugee and migrant backgrounds, both recent arrivals and students who were the children or grandchildren of people caught up in earlier diasporas. Such students might well have been able to draw on other 'funds of knowledge'[8] by thinking about and participating in the simulations. At the same time, the activities would have enabled them and their peers to reflect carefully on the range of factors that contribute towards the movement of people: regime changes, persecution, conflict, famine, poverty, oppression. Being aware of such factors can influence the approaches taken by teachers.

What of the teaching environments and staff that were at students' disposal? Here there were both traditional school classrooms and a museum with galleries, artefacts and large teaching spaces. The staff included the regular teachers but also museum re-enactors – specially trained staff who could act out and dramatize historic roles. For the West Africa trading game in the schools, each village had a table and these were spread around the classroom. The European agent had their own table set up on the edge distinctly separate from the villages (supposedly at the port). It was the Museum enactors who played the roles of merchant prince (dressed flamboyantly) and the European agent (a serious hard-bargaining character).

A similar multi-village layout was adopted for the initial part of the colonial life role-plays. However, furniture was moved to create spaces for larger meetings and the performance of the freeze-frames. This flexibility of classroom space is important as it can help facilitate different pedagogic approaches. The museum – a large and impressive building, buzzing with activity, visitors and all manner of objects – offered very different spaces. The galleries were shared with the public, and so careful thought was needed concerning group sizes and suitable spaces to run the morning activities and utilize real artefacts from West Africa. The Museum education center had big spaces where the groups of 50 were allocated to seven conference tables, each providing a space for the smaller groups to work as a country then be re-organized as a Berlin conference group. The arrangement of these tables in a horseshoe allowed facilitators and teachers to move easily between them, assisting groups as required, and also to address the whole group at key points in the session.

Access to these resources – to particular spaces, to artefacts, to museum staff as well as to teachers – enabled the project to happen. These resources matter: they offer a different range of pedagogic possibilities. But the resources are not, in themselves, sufficient. What also matters is how they are used – and that depends on the adoption of particular approaches to teaching and learning.

Moving to the process variables in the framework, we can start to see how pedagogy is realized. The process variables are summarized as: *'Teacher and student perceptions, strategies and behavior'* and *'characteristics of the learning activities and tasks'*. This is really about what is actually happening in a teaching situation. So what are students (and teachers) doing – and why?

It is clear that the teaching approaches in the History lesson (from the start of this chapter) and in the *Cultures in Contact* project were very different. They start with different assumptions about learning. Rather than assuming the students are passive recipients who simply need knowledge transferred to them, the *Cultures* project seeks to make the students active participants in their own learning. It does this in several ways – and to make this happen pedagogic decisions are required.

A consistent strategy informed the design of the project. Many of the activities required group work that required students to talk to each other. This dialogue was intrinsic to what was happening rather than a 'staged' interaction of question and answer between teacher and student. The activity was devised to require students to make decisions, solve problems, develop group strategies, take action, report on progress and so on. The role play and simulation aspects of the activities meant that sometimes a group 'identity' was formed as students became part of a village or country, thereby both facilitating and requiring from the students greater social interaction and bonding.

In the history lesson the emphasis was almost entirely on the transmission of words (via dictation or copying). In the *Cultures* project, on the other hand, there were photos, pictures, objects, maps, tools (scissors and set squares) and other artefacts. Often students handled these and used them to create new artefacts (trade products, partition maps, freeze frames). So in a sense students were taking ownership (and control) of the education process. They had opportunities to consider different interpretations, to weigh up the evidence, to consult different sources, to ask questions and to develop hypotheses.

The teachers, meanwhile, were taking on facilitator roles during many of the activities. Often the word facilitator implies a kind of passivity – as if this were not really teaching but some lesser form of activity. This was patently not the case here: making the project work required careful planning and resource development; it required knowledge of the students (who might work well, in what roles and groups); and it required clear framing of the activities to provide the suitable balance of knowledge and tasks. Then, when students were undertaking group activities, this needed to be managed to maintain momentum, motivation, direction and a pulling together of component parts to enhance the meaningfulness of what had been happening. In other words, this kind of pedagogy requires substantial prior design and planning as well as interventions in the moment. The teacher's role entails nuanced judgements in addition to careful consideration of the context and process variables. This is in stark contrast to the History lesson, where planning is limited to the selection and production of the information that is to be transferred to the students.

What students might have learned

What of the 'product variables' – effectively the outcomes? We can expect that students will have a better understanding of various aspects of Geography (the make-up, size, location of African states), of History (how imperialism developed over time, how different interests were involved, how a range of different motives and interests coalesced or were in conflict), of Business and Economics (how and why trade occurred).

Yet the *Cultures* students have developed an understanding of these concepts that goes far beyond the memorizing of gobbets of information: the students have constructed their understanding by engaging in a multitude of activities. Because they took part in an activity where they as one European power sought to shape and own parts of Africa for political and economic ends, they are more likely to develop a deeper and more sophisticated understanding of the make-up and size of African states than if they had merely studied and memorized a map.

At the same time as offering a deeper and more critical understanding of curriculum subjects, this teaching approach provides students with opportunities for kinds of learning that are not so easily defined in disciplinary terms. They have learned how to work in teams, argue, compromise, make decisions, how to listen to each other and how to perform. They have learnt about what museums offer and that they can visit them. By taking part in activities within the museum that involved artefacts they have become more than just passive viewers of objects. They have learnt about power and cultural relationships in 19th-century Africa (and Europe). They have gained an insight into how these historic 'cultures in contact' have influenced the make-up of contemporary society (and possibly their own role within it).

It is very difficult to determine with any degree of certainty what learning individuals gain from any teaching. But what the *Cultures in Contact* case study exemplifies is an 'active' pedagogy rather than the 'passive' pedagogy of the History lesson.

This is a vital difference: it dramatizes an important set of arguments: about learning and memory, about the nature of understanding, about the importance of context and previous knowledge. Only partially separable from these arguments is a very simple point: active pedagogies are just more fun. Students get to move about and socialize; because power relationships are less intrusive, they can be more relaxed, more themselves. Their creativity, imagination and humor, rather than being stifled and suppressed, become resources for their learning. All of this is key to motivation and engagement – and learning without motivation and engagement is very difficult, for children and adults alike.

1 Peter Hobson, *The Cradle of Thought: Exploring the Origins of Thinking*, Macmillan, London, 2002; Michael Tomasello, *The Cultural Origins of Human Cognition,* Harvard University Press, Cambridge MA & London, 1999. **2** Jean Lave & Etienne Wenger, *Situated Learning: Legitimate Peripheral Participation*, Cambridge University Press, Cambridge & New York, 1991. **3** Lev Vygotsky, *Problems of General Psychology, including the Volume Thinking and Speech* (trans. N Minick) Plenum, New York & London, 1987, p 170. **4** Nunes et al., *Street mathematics and school mathematics*, Cambridge University Press, Cambridge, 1993. **5** Variables framework adapted from Chris Kyriacou, *Effective Teaching in Schools: Theory and Practice*, Nelson Thornes, Cheltenham, 2009. **6** Resource adapted and developed by Rosa Herxheimer and Adam Unwin from Trading Game, see nin.tl/tradinggameresource **7** lancefuhrer.com/partition_of_africa. htm **8** Gonzalez et al (eds), *Funds of Knowledge: theorizing practices in households, communities, and classrooms*, Lawrence Erlbaum, Mahwah, New Jersey, & London, 2005.

3 Technology is the question, not the answer

'Technology is just a tool. In terms of getting the kids working together and motivating them, the teacher is most important.'

Bill Gates

The claim that technology will transform education is not new – though it seems to carry more weight in an increasingly digital age. But schools can misuse computers as easily as they can reap their benefits. Who has access to the new technology and how is it being used? These questions are just as vital in the era of the smartphone and the tablet as they were when radio and TV were the new kids on the block.

You might be reading this via an ebook on a tablet. This would have been unthinkable just a few years ago. We are in a period of unprecedented, rapid and profound change in the technologies of communication and representation. The extraordinary growth of the internet and mobile technologies has allowed more people very quick access to information. The scope for communication – one-to-one, one-to-many and many-to-many – has been greatly enhanced. These developments have prompted claims and predictions about technology's potential to transform education.

What are the implications of such technologies for learning, for students and the way teaching might be organized? Does technological change determine what education looks like and how it is experienced?

Consider this account by an educator[1] of his visits to two primary schools (with pupils aged between 5 and 11).

Two school visits
Visit One

Today I visited a primary school that was becoming famous for its use of technology.

Our tour started in the nursery, where there were paints, musical instruments, and trays and so on, all in use. In the classrooms there were electronic whiteboards. And in one of these classrooms the teacher was projecting from her computer the numbers 1,2,3 while the class sat on the mat in front of the whiteboard.

In another class, one teacher was projecting on her whiteboard some clip art (perhaps from the internet) which illustrated aspects of the story the whole class were working on.

Each teaching area had an extra space next to its group of classrooms. In total these had 10 children in them when I visited, out of a school of 700.

Another class teacher was using the whiteboard to draw on, using the computer 'pens', as her way of demonstrating the worksheet task to the class.

There were some similar examples of the teacher using the whiteboard and a computer to work with the whole class.

In a central area of the school building were two suites of newly installed computers, about 12 or more per room. I was told that these had been donated and that now the school had become a regional training center to train teachers in word processing, spreadsheets and presentational software. I mused with my guide that these were business-oriented software packages, and that the industrial donor probably didn't understand educational software, but she didn't seem to understand my point.

In summary:
- I never saw a pupil use a computer;
- I only saw teachers use a computer;
- I saw rooms of computers not being used;
- I only saw whole class teaching;
- I saw no educational software.

The architecture and design were stunning, there was

a quiet atmosphere throughout the school, and I was told that half a million pounds had been allocated to computer purchase before opening.

I ended up wondering whether I had seen a Victorian model of teaching and learning dressed up with a little new technology.

Visit Two

Today I visited a primary school that was becoming famous for its use of technology.

We passed storerooms which had been converted to house half a dozen computers.

Two pupils at each computer worked away busily. In the corridor there were occasional desks outside a classroom where another computer stood, each with another pair of pupils.

In the first classroom, a group of about 10 children were grouped around a computer with screen projection. In turn they took control of the keyboard and mouse to ensure that they had all learned to cut and paste text between two windows for a story they were working on. They didn't respond to the interruption of the visitors. Above them were posters about VIPs – very independent persons, and what such learners might do when they finished their work or when they got stuck. In another corner of the room two other pupils worked at another keyboard.

On the way back down the corridor, I went into one of the converted store-rooms and asked a student what he was doing. He demonstrated to me a computer presentation he was just finishing on our responses to refugees: it was technically engaging and personally moving. He then volunteered (with apparent pride) 'I'm a computer tutor' and explained how he helped his peers.

In the nursery, students were learning how to program the movements of a computer-drive 'turtle'.

Back in another class there was no sign of any student working on a computer: groups of four to six students were working on a range of collaborative tasks, ranging from artwork to literacy tasks to some number problems.

In other classes, various sub-groups again were working on a variety of tasks, while in the corner three or four were working on a revision site on the internet.

At the end of the visit we were taken to a special suite where the computers seemed to have higher-level software: some students were invited to demonstrate some of the features. One pupil showed me how he had built up a portfolio of his work, and how one part of it included data on his progress through the school: this was to be written onto CD for him to take as his record of achievement to secondary school. I said to him that the software packages that he had been using were mainly presentational ones: he said 'Yes, but it's good to be skilled on those – there are other things on some websites we use'.

In summary:
- I never saw a teacher use a computer;
- I only saw pupils use a computer;
- I saw rooms of pupils working without immediate supervision;
- I only saw paired and small-group teaching;
- I saw a range of software, including educational.

There was an engaged 'buzz' throughout the school, and I did not hear a single teacher say 'desist' (Stop that, shut up, etc.) the whole day.

I was told that the government inspectors had particularly remarked that in the staff room the teachers talked about learning.

I ended up thinking I had seen a transformed school.

What is an educational technology?

It is often assumed that educational technologies are something modern and involve computers. But as long as formal education has taken place, teachers have sought methods, equipment and resources to help them teach. Is an aid to teaching also an aid to learning? This is something to bear in mind as we consider how various technologies are used in education.

 Rethinking education

One way to define an educational technology is that it is anything beyond the actual people present in the classroom. Textbooks spring to mind as an obvious example, since they have been and continue to be immensely influential in shaping conceptions of pedagogy, knowledge and curriculum.

Also included in this category are everyday items such as pens, paper and books. Because of their ubiquity, they are less likely to be viewed as tools for teaching – although of course teaching and learning would be different without them. We tend to think of writing, say, as a single activity, and one that is primarily to do with language. But writing always involves the manipulation of physical resources. Writing with a pencil is not quite the same as writing with a fountain pen, which is also different from writing with a biro. What writing feels like – and what it represents culturally – can also be affected by the quality of the paper: jotting on the back of a betting slip does not afford the same tactile pleasure as writing on vellum. And writing on paper is substantially different from writing with chalk on a slate. Each set of material resources offers different possibilities, different limitations – and each has a set of different meanings and associations that accumulate through a history of practice.

On the other hand, equipment such as desks, display boards and markers are very much associated with classrooms. Indeed, they are essential elements in the stereotypical image of a classroom – the one with neat rows of desks all facing towards the front where the teacher has a desk and a display board. Then there are variations on this: the science lab, with very fixed workbenches, sinks and various science-specific equipment; the technology workshop; the ICT suite, and so on.

The classroom environment is where technologies shape teaching and learning – and where culturally specific ideas about learning and teaching shape the ways in which technologies are deployed. If the classroom is set up with rows of desks all facing the board, then it foregrounds a transmission-type pedagogy (similar to 'The History lesson' in the last chapter). Teachers command a center-stage position, they are the focus of attention, they are in control, they will be inclined to adopt teacher-centered methods and use the board to help the transmission. And this use of these common classroom technologies (desks and display boards) tends to seem normal – natural, even – to us, partly because such a disposition of resources has a long history. If we look at images of 19th-century classrooms this is the layout we find. The large numbers of students in a typical classroom meant this might have been justified as the best use of space available, but it was also a design that accorded with the dominant pedagogy of transmission and rote learning in that era. Today, even in contexts where there may be smaller class sizes and more nuanced understandings of the way people learn, such classroom layouts remain the default.

The traditional layout of the classroom persists because that is what schooling looks like; in other words, there are powerful cultural assumptions at work. These assumptions have an effect on how newer technologies are incorporated into schooling. So, for example, there is considerable evidence of interactive whiteboards being used precisely as older whiteboards, or blackboards, had been used – as sites of display, not interaction, as hi-tech tools for a very old teacher-centered approach. This also raises the question of the relation between technology, pedagogy and power: newer technologies have often been co-opted in the service of existing hierarchies of power and knowledge.

The layout of the room – and the place of technologies within it – facilitates and normalizes certain teaching approaches and constrains others. What if the teacher wanted students to talk to each other or work in groups or if they wanted to move around, monitor and help individuals? The traditional classroom environment makes this difficult.

Yet desks do not have to be rigid and fixed in rows. Rarely do modern desks, which are simply small tables, have storage facilities. They can be moved around to provide all kinds of different layouts. Think back to the 'Cultures in contact' project in the last chapter. One classroom was set up to represent villages and traders in West Africa in the 19th century; another the Berlin Conference role play as part of the Scramble for Africa. Such arrangements were key to achieving active forms of teaching and learning as well as to encouraging student dialogue and participation.

The possibilities of technology

The starting position, then, is neither dismissive of, nor infatuated with, technologies. Access to resources opens up possibilities for teaching and learning but we can never assume that the introduction of a technology to the educational process is automatically an improvement on what went before.

The simplistic view that technology is always beneficial to education has a long history. In 1922 Thomas Edison, the famous inventor of, among other things, the light bulb and movie camera, claimed: 'The motion picture is destined to revolutionize our education system and... in a few years it will supplant largely, if not entirely, the use of textbooks.' In 1945 William Levenson, then director of the Ohio School of the Air, said: 'The time may come when a portable radio receiver will be as common in the classroom as is the blackboard.'

One can understand their enthusiasm at the advent of a technology that offered a new form of mass communication. Such technological optimism continued as television and video recording usage became more widespread. There was a conviction that education would be enriched, that students would learn more and faster (and teachers teach less). And this rosy view of educational technologies is still very much with us today. It informs the policy of some of the most powerful global interests in education, as we will see in Chapter 6.

Why the promise of many of these new technologies remained unfulfilled is not reducible to a single explanation. There were practical, logistical problems with teachers and classes having access to the equipment, and knowing how to use it. If equipment broke, repairs were often slow. But there has also been a tendency, already alluded to above, for teachers to assimilate new technologies within their existing pedagogic repertoires. In some cases, this tendency was encouraged by the nature of the technologies themselves.

Broadcast media (radio, film, television) are by definition transmission technologies: they offer one-way communication. They provide material for a mass audience, a 'one size fits all' approach that might sit most comfortably within a transmission pedagogy, thereby discouraging teachers from developing approaches to meet the needs or address the interests of a particular group of students. This is not to undervalue such media – numerous TV, film and radio productions have huge potential for learning – but it does indicate that there is work to be done by the teacher if these resources are to be mediated in ways that might enable this potential to be exploited (see box on 'edutainment').

But what about computers?

In the 1980s the first desktop computers started to be introduced to schools. Soon most large and secondary schools in the Global North would have dedicated computer rooms. These precious technologies (they were relatively expensive) were often in high demand, so subjects were in competition for computer-room time. Use was often dominated by Mathematics and Science, then later by Computing, Information Technology (IT) and Business, as these subjects and computer appli-cations grew. Rarely were computers used regularly

Edutainment

Technologies such as radio and television enabled the production of serial dramas with educational messages. These have been used in countries with limited access to formal schooling. In 1993, for example, a radio drama *Twende na Wakati* was aired in Tanzania to promote education about family planning and HIV infection – rather as the long-running British BBC radio serial *The Archers* had originally been designed in the 1950s to help farmers keep up to date with developments.

More recently, animated computer games and the internet have increased the availability and changed the nature of edutainment. Rather than implementing a public-service agenda, these are more about maximizing sales in a highly competitive and lucrative market. An educational tag might be used as part of a marketing strategy.

How educational are such games? The plethora of what is available means it would be foolish to generalize. Certainly some have developed sophisticated use of simulations and role plays to engage users with concepts – as with those that concern the development of cities or other socio-economic communities. There are also those that require communication between participants and involve creating online gaming communities.

In other circumstances games like these might be educationally useful, allowing problem solving, dialogue, joint enterprise and a learner voice. With typical games software, though, this is limited: there are inevitably prescribed outcomes (even if there are a lot of them) and no opportunity to critique these.

Implicit in much of this edutainment are questionable values and stereotyping. This can involve fostering sexualized images of female protagonists (think of Lara Croft), using race and ethnicity in negative and violent roles, even the representation of localities/countries as dangerous and undesirable. Typical objectives are to win or to accumulate wealth often at the cost of others.

Children can see games for what they are and not as representations of reality. Nevertheless, reinforcing negative stereotypes, being culturally insensitive and promoting particular ways of behaving (even in a game) is problematic – particularly without the scope to discuss, challenge and consider alternatives that is an intrinsic part of positive learning.

or integrated into subject teaching. Primary schools, because of their smaller size and limited budgets (and because of assumptions about where the technology fitted into the curriculum) had limited exposure to computers.

In this early phase, rather than spreading out the computers among existing teaching spaces (with one per classroom, say) the 'high security' computer suite dominated. Using computers was special rather than being integrated into everyday teaching and learning. Much of what went on in the computer suite was about learning how to use the machines, from the keyboard to various programs – an approach, in other words, that focused on the acquisition of skills rather than concepts. There was also the tendency for the software to be business-oriented rather than specifically educational.

These new computer rooms required changes in classroom layout, and hence in teaching approach. It did not work to have rows of desks (with computers on) facing the front. Teachers and students could not see and communicate with each other properly. Cabling and power supply also influenced layout. Rooms tended to be organized with computers around the edge with all screens facing the middle of the room, sometimes with an additional central bank of computers if space allowed.

This layout did not facilitate traditional whole-class teaching, since students were sitting in front of a computer, behind which was a wall, rather than facing towards a single focal point, occupied by the teacher and the board. The layout – and the prestige attached to the equipment – meant that the lesson became oriented towards acquiring the skills of using the computer, with teachers moving around, helping students, dealing with problems as they arose. All these factors led to more individualized or small-group approaches within the classroom.

Materials were designed to allow students to progress at their own pace and be supported by the teacher. The teacher became more of a facilitator, the power relationship less marked in individual conversations about a third party (the computer/software). Earlier we suggested that the technologies of rigid rows of desks and display boards encouraged transmission-type teaching. Here, though, the technology encouraged a different approach – one that, in general, privileged individual learning and activity, with relatively little scope for collaboration among pupils.

...and the internet?

From the mid-1990s onwards, the internet reached into many aspects of everyday life. In education, this new era was reflected in the insertion of the term 'communication' into the phrase 'Information and Communication Technology' (ICT) – computers were no longer seen as a means of storing and processing information, and became communicational resources.

The development of ICT has continued unabated. Internet access is widespread, at least in more affluent countries, often with wireless availability. ICT equipment has become more portable. Mobile phones have become more like computers and computers more like mobile phones. For the owners of such devices the amount of information available is vast and often very quick to access.

What are the implications of this for education and learning? Predictions were that it would be 'transformational'. World leaders were keen to align themselves with the modernizing vision it offered education. US President Bill Clinton announced the 'absolutely astonishing transformation; a moment of great possibility' (1996), while UK Prime Minister Tony Blair declared that 'Technology has transformed the way we work and is now set to transform the way we learn' (1997).

Transformation implies change beyond recognition, a completely new way of doing things. That the new technologies of communication and representation have had a profound impact on us is beyond dispute; whether the rhetoric of transformation is apt is less clear. It is worth looking carefully at aspects of continuity as well as of change – and to consider the gains and losses. Online shopping, for example, is very different from face-to-face shopping. It is less physical, less social and less public. But it still requires looking at different products and making choices – and it still entails the exchange of money for goods as part of a wider economic system marked by massive structural inequalities.

So how has learning been transformed? Certainly, the new technologies have enabled much wider access to almost unlimited information. But this information (like all information, derived from any source) is always mediated, filtered, processed. Take the web search. We need to understand that search engines such as Google and Yahoo rank (and thus influence) the information presented – they render some information more readily accessible than other information (often in return for payment). And then there is the issue of how students (or indeed any of us) make selections from this unlimited mass of information, what use they make of it, how they evaluate it. This depends on what they know already, how the information is presented, their motivations, their interests, their contexts and many other factors.

Virtual learning

The same issues occur in relation to the use of these technologies in more formal education contexts such as schools. Virtual learning environments (VLE) are constructed for the purposes of communicating with students and providing downloadable learning resources. These can become depositories of one-size-fits-all presentations, thus creating another version of transmission teaching, with the onus on the students merely to download and engage with the materials. They tend to be doing this individually, with fewer opportunities for dialogue with teachers or peers. The learner is here re-imagined as the receiver of content. Such learning technologies are often very attractive to policymakers and managers: they promise low-cost, scalable solutions as well as a high degree of centralized control.

When we think of communication, we usually envisage it as a two-way process. The ways in which VLEs are configured and used, however, often creates communication that is as unidirectional as in the traditional transmission classroom: from the 'expert' to the student. To create genuinely interactive ways for students to raise issues, discuss concepts, and solve problems can be difficult, especially if the course is 'rolled' out to many students, often at a distance. The online learning environments of the 21st century can be every bit as constraining as the rigid desks and huge class sizes of the 19th. Technological advances are no guarantor of progressive teaching methods.

Technologies are neither worthless nor inimical to dialogue. They have huge potential to enhance learning in many ways, involving many more people. But the learners, their context, their previous understanding, their motivations and their social interactions: all of these are essential factors in any worthwhile learning process. They are not to be neglected. Because of this, you should be suspicious of simplistic claims about the value of hi-tech, 'one size fits all' approaches to mass education.

Technology adoption

Practices, whether individual or institutional, develop over time. Marc Prensky coined the terms 'digital native' and 'digital immigrant' to discriminate between those born into in a digital, media-saturated world and those that need to adapt to it.[2] Claims have been made that this new generation thinks and processes information in a different way, that 'digital natives' need a media-rich learning environment to hold their attention. The extent to which this generational digital divide exists is questionable. A plethora of factors – wealth, aptitude, motivation and exposure, for instance – influence how individuals adapt to and use technology.

To explore the potential and the challenges of adopting new technologies, it is worth exploring some specific examples. As with the two school visits at the start of this chapter, one needs to look below the surface. Prensky suggests that there is what he calls a 'typical process of technology adoption' while warning that 'schools are not typical of anything'. The four steps are:

- Dabbling with technology (random, inconsistent and experimental use)
- Doing old things in old ways (the teacher presents students with writing on a screen and asks them to copy this into their books)
- Doing old things in new ways (the teacher annotates a piece of text on screen, rather than on acetate or a blackboard)
- Doing new things in new ways (using technology to do things that were not possible before)

These four versions of technology adoption may sometimes occur as steps – as stages in the exploration of what a new technology enables people to do. But they can also be found alongside one another, even coexisting in the same classroom. Prensky's model may be useful in thinking critically about what is happening in these examples.

The 'Hole in the Wall' project

In 1999, a research team led by Sugata Mitra set up a computer in a very poor part of Delhi, India, with a camera to film what was happening.[3] It was located in a wall with the screen visible from the street. It had internet access and some other programs as well as a mouse/touchpad. No instructions were given; it was available for anyone who wanted to use it. Children started using the computer enthusiastically. These children had little or no formal education and the internet was not commonplace. Yet within a few months many of them had learned how to use the computer (they had learned, for example, how to maneuver the mouse/touchpad, to open and employ software, to create, save and reuse files) and they could access the internet. When they were asked how they had learnt to do this, they said they had taught themselves.

The team set up two other computers: one in another city, one in a rural location. The same learning happened without any assistance. Since then the project has expanded and run in many areas of India and other countries. The team has researched these as examples of self-directed learning. Their main observations of the learning processes have been that:

- Working in groups is important.
- The children explore ways to use the computer, often making accidental discoveries.
- Children show each other how things work.
- New learners often repeat the processes several times.
- They develop a shared language to describe what is happening and help explain things to each other.
- There will be children who 'know' more than others, and this information is shared freely in return for friendship or other information. They do not feel they 'own' the information as they might some property.

What does this case tell us about technology and learning? It is clear that the technology had a motivating role. There was the novelty element – a new technology that they are aware of but have never had the chance to try out. It was a community asset rather than part of a formal education system, so there were no classrooms, no teachers, no rules (other than the rules they agreed on themselves).

What of the learning? The participants were curious, interested in finding out how things work and how they can use it to find out other things. There were elements of problem-solving and discovery. Important, too, was the collaborative nature of the activities. As was argued in Chapter 2, 'humans are irreducibly social animals'. The way the children showed each other and worked together was central to the learning processes. The learning and knowledge was not seen as 'owned' by anyone; there was a recognition that it was beneficial to share and construct knowledge together. What the technology provided was a vehicle and focus.

The project has moved on to promote the use of what is termed 'self-organized learning environments'. There is an emphasis on helping communities that suffer from 'remoteness' – areas that are remote because they are very rural or because of acute urban poverty. Formal educational provision is weaker in these areas for many reasons. Providing community technological resources (along 'hole in the wall' principles) can supplement and enhance the learning that happens in schools.

While this project was innovative and raised many questions about how learning happens, we should nonetheless resist the urge to regard it as a panacea. More detailed work could be done on who used the resources, whether it was dominated by particular groups and whether others were excluded. Was the hierarchy of existing power and gender relations reproduced in these activities?

The next case moves to a more affluent country, the UK. It concerns children of primary-school age in inner-city schools.

The primary school bloggers

This was a research project that ran in three London schools in 2012.[4] The researchers were interested in the differences between blog writing and traditional school writing in exercise books. Each class was covering typical primary-school curriculum topics and activities. The difference was that they were using a class blog to which all the pupils contributed in addition to writing in their individual exercise books. They used and developed their expertise on many of the blogging functions, such as having their own mini blog area and incorporating pictures and videos. The blogs were 'open access', which meant they could work on them from home, they could show their families what they had been doing and so on. The children were enthusiastic about blogging. They liked the fact that there was a wider audience than just school:

there was excitement if someone commented, especially if that someone was from another country.

What students were asked to do was well framed: they were asked to write in a role (as a news reporter, for example) or for a particular audience. The blog work reported on and developed ideas from class activities about a topic. So one class was learning about the Vikings (journeys, gods and goddesses, and so on). They had a Viking day where they dressed up as Vikings, took part in mock battles and used 'freeze-frames' to act out key events. They took photographs and used these with comic-book software to add captions and speech bubbles. This then became part of the class blog about the Vikings. They participated in these activities as groups and made collaborative decisions about what to include and how to present their content in their class blog.

Teachers reported that the blogging enhanced relationships between school and home. Students were sharing with the school community more about their home life and family members became more aware (and interested) in what they were doing at school. The teachers felt that the blogs had increased pupils' engagement in writing: a growth in writing confidence, a greater awareness of audience, of genre and an improved sense of their writer voice. They gained a better understanding of their own writing and that of others and saw themselves as part of a writing community.

The context here and how the technology is used are different from the 'hole in the wall' project. It starts in a formal schooling situation, with a particular curriculum of topics to be learnt, and with the specific aim of developing the students' writing. There was not an instant improvement in writing (considered as the acquisition of isolable writing skills) as a consequence of the introduction of a technology. What happened was that the blogs encouraged learning in many ways – and a different orientation towards writing. The technology in this case was used to create a joint enterprise (the class blog). This joint enterprise went out to a wider audience. This 'publishing' motivated them, the feedback from families and others providing a form of praise and sense of achievement beyond normal teacher feedback. A joint enterprise such as this requires students to work together: they cannot achieve this without discussion, arguments, sharing and mediating each other's ideas.

Some of the attributes of this learning are similar to the 'active' approaches in the *Cultures in Contact* project from Chapter 2. There are also distinct differences; with the class blog, the joint enterprise was more long term, the students had more creative control, it was more 'owned' by the class. It became integrated into different aspects of their school work rather than being a 'one off' relatively short-term activity focusing on one curriculum area. Whereas some of the technologies discussed earlier tended to reinforce a transmission approach, here the technology expanded the options rather than restricting them.

It might be tempting to decide that all we need to do is to set up class blogs and enhanced learning will follow. But teachers were vital to the success of this project. They thought about how to frame what the students were required to do on the blog, planned and provided resources, organized pupil groupings from their knowledge of who worked with whom, advised on how the blog worked, set up the room and equipment, provided group and individual feedback and so on. Such teachers' decisions remind us of the importance of considering the context and process variables that exist in any classroom.

The research also found that the class blog enabled teachers to understand more about students outside school (such as their interests, activities, families and culture). It is an example of how a particular approach can not only help students learn, but also help the teacher to understand them better. The more a teacher knows about her students, the more able she is to support their progress. She is in a better position to empathize, to motivate, to engage by using this more nuanced knowledge of students in their teaching approaches.

The next two case studies take off in a slightly different direction, looking at the provision of technological resources and access to the internet in Africa and considering more global influences on education.

Worldreader: Ghana

The non-profit organization Worldreader describes its aims as follows: 'Literacy is transformative: it increases earning potential, decreases inequality, improves health outcomes and breaks the cycle of poverty. Yet there are 740 million illiterate people in this world and 250 million children of primary-school age who lack basic reading and writing skills. Books are necessary for the development of these skills, and still 50 per cent of schools in Africa have few or no books at all. Worldreader is on a mission to bring digital books to every child and her family, so that they can improve their lives.' [5]

The idea is that e-readers such as a 'Kindle' or mobile device can be used to supply digital books to poor communities. It is recognized that capacity must be developed to support this initiative, which is usually taken up by schools or libraries. For example, local phone providers are trained to repair devices.

The Ghanaian education system is based around books. The problem is they are expensive, in short supply (they have to be shared between many students) and those available wear out. The e-readers are entry-level, robust, low in power consumption and need no internet connection, but can store up to 5,000 books.

Worldreader recognizes the danger of the digital colonialism that would be the by-product of having only Western ebooks. So, working with publishers, they are developing a range of African-originated books. Their aim is to scale up as technology prices fall. They claim that, as books are a familiar technology, their project is more readily accepted by the teachers and students involved.

Wikimedia: South Africa

Wikimedia is part of the Wikipedia group. It is a global movement whose aim is to bring free educational content to the world. In 2013 students from a township outside Cape Town wrote an open letter to mobile operators requesting free access to Wikipedia on their mobile phones. They explained the difficulties they had with access in their libraries and schools. Later that year, one large mobile operator made Wikipedia access free for all of its 20 million users.

As this kind of access grows, Wikimedia recognizes a number of priorities. One challenge is that currently most of its contributions come from and are used in North America and Europe. Wikimedia understands that this can cause systematic bias. It does not want its wider global users just to be 'content consumers'; they want educators and students to participate. They have developed programs to support them in providing local content, some of it in local languages.

These cases are concerned with providing access to existing information and having the tools to do this. In a sense, this reflects the policy initiatives taken by more affluent countries around the Millennium (such as the information superhighway in the US or the National Grid for Learning in the UK). There was considerable investment in providing equipment and connecting schools to the internet, on the assumption that the equipment and connection would transform learning. But these two African examples of digital innovation are actually rather different from the earlier developments. They may be more modest in scope, but they are also much more finely attuned to local circumstance. They seek to address deficiencies in existing provision – deficiencies identified by participants in particular communities and education systems. Technology here is responsive to need; it enables existing forms of education to work better. And it is introduced in ways that are politically accountable, that recognize and seek to address problems in representation. Both cases recognize that it is a problem if all resources are provided by the Global North. This awareness of cultural imperialism matters.

Social media and 'digital natives'

We live in increasingly 'digitally' connected societies. Smartphone ownership is already commonplace across the globe. The implications for education and learning are unclear. As with several of the earlier debates in this chapter, we should be cautious about making false claims.

Nevertheless, it is worth considering these learners (and future learners) – these 'digital natives' growing up in this world where they are constantly digitally connected to their families, their friends, wider interest groups and to the informational resources of the internet. A recurrent argument of this book is that dialogue between learners is important, that humans are inherently social animals, and that social interaction – asking questions, explaining ideas – is key to learning. One would then expect these enhanced opportunities for communication to be positive for learning. There are many gains for learners in their capacity to be part of social networks and multiple – overlapping – communities. They can rapidly and continuously share ideas, recount experiences, raise problems, voice opinions, get feedback and so on.

Could there be possible downsides of being constantly connected to what are in essence semi-public social networks? Recent research concerning smartphone and internet use highlights potential issues. Being digitally connected is often used to provide social comfort (being part of networks).[6] This can, however, lead to increased feelings of loneliness – being more aware of what others are doing that you are not part of. It also tends to be addictive and to provide constant distractions that lower concentration and enhance the tendency to avoid tasks.

Some of these issues will be familiar to observers

of multitasking digital natives. One can set this within a global context of fast capitalism, where immediacy, rolling news and superficial soundbites are in the forefront. Is it surprising that some of these young learners struggle with deferred gratification and concentration? In their online lives, they may not be learning to mull things over, to ruminate, to participate in more extended and more demanding dialogue.

Perhaps, then, there is still a role for the face-to-face interactions of school.

1 Chris Watkins, nin.tl/watkinsICT **2** Marc Prensky, nin.tl/Prenskytech **3** Sugata Mitra Hole-in-the-Wall Education, hole-in-the-wall.com/Beginnings. html **4** Myra Barrs and Sarah Horrocks, *Educational blogs and their effects on pupils' writing*. CfBT, London, 2014, nin.tl/CFBTresearch **5** worldreader. org/what-we-do **6** LJ Hadlington, 'Cognitive failures in daily life: Exploring the link with Internet addiction and problematic mobile phone use,' *Computers in Human Behavior*, 51, 2015.

4 Knowledge, curriculum and control

'One cannot expect positive results from an educational
or political action program which fails to respect the
particular view of the world held by the people. Such a
program constitutes cultural invasion, good intentions
notwithstanding.'

Paolo Freire

**Who decides what is taught in schools? In the past
this was largely left to teachers but governments
increasingly see this as their responsibility. Yet any
curriculum comes laden with sets of values and
assumptions – and the students' interests can be
one of the lowest priorities.**

If children and young people go to school to learn, what
exactly are they meant to learn there? The concept of
a curriculum is a way of answering this question. The
word 'curriculum' is etymologically close to the word
'course': a course of study, like a racecourse, involves
a starting point, movement over time, and a finishing
point. So a curriculum can be understood as a plan or
outline of what is to be learnt.

You could argue that it is precisely the existence of
a curriculum in this sense, as a plan, that distinguishes
school learning from out-of-school learning. Whereas the
latter tends to be spontaneous, unpredictable, responsive
to events and experiences and largely led by the learner's
interests, school learning is structured, planned for and
determined, for the most part, from on high.

Already, this description of a curriculum raises two
vital questions. First, does the existence of a curriculum
mean that learning inside school is fundamentally, qual-
itatively, different from learning in the world outside?
Second, who makes decisions about the curriculum and
how are such decisions made?

As Chapter 2 suggested, there is no evidence that the learning that is accomplished in classrooms involves different processes from the learning that happens elsewhere. Learning is a complicated, messy and intensely social process, in which the interests of the learner are always a powerful factor. Because of this, a curriculum in this sense of the term – a course plan– is not the same thing at all as an account of what will be, or has been, learnt. A curriculum cannot simply be delivered, like a sack of rice.

The second question – who decides? – has become increasingly fraught in recent decades. In many parts of the world, national governments have taken the power to prescribe the content of the curriculum. This assertion of central control over what is to be taught (and, it is usually assumed, over what is to be learnt) has been justified in all kinds of ways: to meet the needs of the national economy; to provide a more highly skilled workforce; to raise standards; to make schools accountable for the education that they provide and to achieve consistency and coherence in teaching across different schools; to ensure equal access to knowledge, or to the benefits that schooling, or qualifications, might provide; to enable all to become full citizens and active, responsible participants in society. Often, governments have offered several of these reasons simultaneously – even though they are premised on very different under-standings of what a curriculum, or indeed a school, is for.

Designing a curriculum involves making choices about what is included, and therefore, inevitably, about what is excluded. It involves making decisions about what is appropriate for all learners, or about what might be appropriate for some learners (and not others). Likewise, any curriculum is based on beliefs about values and purposes – about what is worth knowing, about which skills are worth acquiring, about what education is for. It is not surprising, then, that questions of curriculum design and content have been – and continue to be – highly contentious.

Dividing the curriculum into subjects

A curriculum is always a construct – in other words, it is not handed down in tablets of stone but rather is something that human beings have made. But curriculum designers do not start with a blank slate; they cannot, because they are themselves products of educational systems, and thus imbued with the culture, values and assumptions that are encoded in such systems. For example, curricula tend to be organized around, and segmented into, a series of separate subjects: mathematics, science, history, geography, language arts, creative and expressive arts, religious and physical education, and so on.

This way of organizing the curriculum is so deeply embedded in schooling that it seems natural. It isn't. It represents a particular way of parcelling up knowledge into different subjects, or disciplines, that is relatively recent – a product of the past couple of centuries or so. To a large extent, too, this approach to knowledge was first institutionalized in universities, in the creation of separate 'faculties', and then transferred downwards from universities to schools – though the relation between academic disciplines and school subjects is more complex, and more varied, than this bald summary might suggest.

As disciplinary knowledge has become institutionalized and, within universities, increasingly specialized, schooling has tended to be understood as the acquisition of knowledge in a series of separate subjects, while the subjects themselves appear as fixed entities, each with its own set of procedures and each with its own body of knowledge. And this view of the curriculum fits in neatly with the idea, discussed in Chapter 2, of education as a process of transmission.

This model has its advantages – and its fervent

adherents. It makes the processes of planning and organization more manageable, since the curriculum can be parcelled up into separate subjects, with different people responsible for determining what gets taught in each. Such a curriculum corresponds closely, too, with many secondary teachers' sense of themselves and their professional identity: it is common for secondary-school teachers to see themselves as possessing expertise in relation to their subject: they are teachers of mathematics, or art, or French. And it can be argued that the different subjects and their associated disciplines represent different ways of engaging with the world, different ways of addressing different problems. The questions that a historian asks, and how she might go about answering them, are not the same as the puzzles that a physicist confronts, and how she might investigate them. The divisions between disciplines, in other words, are not simply arbitrary, and schooling can be regarded as a means of inducting learners into these ways of exploring ourselves and the world about us.

But there are a number of problems with this model. First, and most fundamental, it encourages the view of knowledge as something that exists in its own right, separate from human activity, from the processes of knowing and understanding. Knowledge can thus seem to be merely sets of facts, to be ingested (the Gradgrind model of education). But knowledge is never quite so impersonal, quite so abstract. It is always embedded in human history and culture, always a product of human interests and motives. Facts are never separable from meanings, whether those facts are notable dates (say 1917, the year of the Russian Revolution) or mathematical and scientific formulae (πr^2 or $e=mc^2$). And meanings are always made, never simply handed on.

Second, it treats the disciplines, or school subjects, as unchanging. This is deeply misleading, in that it obscures both the extent to which they are themselves products of historical processes and the fact that they remain contested, shifting and unstable domains. Geography, for example, is not neatly separable from history or science, from economics or politics, while it is not at all clear if it is still possible to regard biology as distinct from chemistry. In school, there is a tendency to treat subjects as separate from each other, and from the world beyond the school gates. That is, of course, how the subjects appear on a secondary student's timetable: Tuesday morning, Biology; Wednesday afternoon, Geography. One effect of this is to discourage students from making connections between their learning in different areas of the curriculum – and this is a pity, since such connections can in themselves be powerful engines of learning.

Third, there is a huge and largely unacknowledged gulf between the intellectual disciplines and the school subjects, a gulf that is all the more remarkable given that they often share the same name. A very clear example of this was provided in an experiment conducted a quarter of a century ago by the US academic Sam Wineburg.

History and school history: worlds apart

Wineburg's experiment involved eight professional historians and eight high-school students.[1] The professional historians had widely different areas of special interest; the high school students were all high-achieving and had all chosen history courses. Each participant was presented with a series of documents relating to the Battle of Lexington, an episode in the American Revolutionary War. The documents ranged from first-hand accounts to a school textbook and a fictional treatment of the battle. The participants were asked to do two things: first, to provide a spoken commentary (thinking aloud, as it were) while they read the documents, so that their thought processes, their immediate responses to the texts, could be recorded; second, to rank the documents in order of their trustworthiness.

What emerged from this experiment was a startling

difference between the two groups. The historians ranked the school textbook as the least trustworthy of all the documents, even less reliable than the fictional account. The high-school students, on the other hand, rated the school textbook as the most reliable of all.

Why was this? The think-aloud process revealed that the historians and the high-school students were reading the documents in different ways, for entirely different purposes. For the high-school students, reading was a process of comprehension, of getting at the facts; when the historians read the documents, they were inter-rogating them to establish what the text was trying to do. The students paid little attention to the identity and motives of the writer or to the text's intended audience or purposes; for the historians, these questions were vital, framing their reading of the words on the page.

As Wineburg argues, these are not just differences in reading strategies; they reveal fundamental differences between the two groups' understandings of what history is, of what it means to engage in the practice of history. In high school, it would appear that history is about identifying and recalling facts; for historians, it is about asking questions.

This gap between school subjects and the disciplines with which they are associated is problematic. School students should be encouraged to ask big questions, to approach the evidence critically and to see knowledge as always provisional, always contested. It is patronizing – and actually deeply anti-educational – to flatten out, sanitize and distort what it is that historians do so as to create a shrink-wrapped, ersatz package called 'school history'.

There are those who argue that this gap between subject and discipline, between what happens in school and what happens in university, is both necessary and beneficial – that students need to learn the facts before they can begin to engage intellectually with the questions that are addressed within a discipline.

Wineburg's research helps to show what is wrong with this approach. It is hard to see how this version of school history could possibly be considered as an appropriate preparation for the practice of history. Moreover, any experience of teaching in schools soon reveals that it doesn't have to be like this. It is perfectly possible to enable young people to experience the intellectual challenges and rewards of the discipline itself. Why give children thin gruel when much richer, more interesting, more nourishing food is available?

Content versus skills

One form that the argument over the curriculum has taken is in a polarized debate about content and skills. Should the process of designing a curriculum start with the specification of what is to be learnt (the content) or with the methods and aptitudes that will be developed (the skills)? Cultural conservatives such as the hugely influential ED Hirsch[2] have tended to emphasize content; some progressives, and also those who see education as primarily a preparation for the world of work, have favored a skills-based approach. Wineburg's findings might be construed as an indication that the high-school students had a view of history as a body of content, whereas the professional historians' approach exemplified history as method, as mode of inquiry.

Another way of representing this is the difference between *knowing that* and *knowing how*. Is it more useful for students to know that the Amritsar Massacre happened in 1919, or that they know how to interrogate a contemporary account of the atrocity? Is it more important that they know hydrogen to be an element with a single positively charged proton and a single negatively charged electron, or that they understand how to analyze the properties of different elements?

An exclusive focus on *knowing that* – the Gradgrind approach – is an inadequate basis for curriculum design. There are, however, dangers in approaches that so privilege skills (*knowing how*) as to present a curriculum lacking any specific content. Historians become better at reading documentary evidence by reading particular documents, relating to particular events. Content is, after all, what tends to excite people's interest. And might some content be more interesting – more valuable, even – than other content?

Linked to this is the concept of an *entitlement curriculum* – a curriculum that represents the knowledge and skills to which all people, as humans and also, perhaps, as members of a particular society, are entitled to have access. Such knowledge and skills, it might be argued, are essential for full participation in society, and thus it becomes necessary for an individual to acquire them in order to thrive. At this level of generality, this view of curriculum as a universal right seems quite attractive. It becomes somewhat trickier, though, at a concrete level.

What do we mean by literacy?

We might, for example, all agree that literacy is a good thing, and that an essential part of a school's responsibility is to ensure that all children acquire it. But what do we mean by literacy? What it is to be literate has meant, and continues to mean, vastly different things at different moments in history and in different societies. It sometimes means being able to make the right sounds when confronted with a bit of text. And there have been times when being able to make these sounds was a matter of life and death.

In England, from medieval times at least until the 17th century, a member of the clergy could not be condemned to death for his first capital offense. Instead, he would be branded on the hand or thumb — M for murder, T for theft (so that he couldn't get away with a second offense). This 'benefit of clergy' was extended to anyone who could read. The courts determined whether the accused was literate or not by giving him a reading test.

The test passage was usually the first verse of Psalm 51 ('Have mercy upon me, oh God, according to thy loving kindness; according unto the multitude of thy tender mercies, blot out my transgressions'), which was known as the 'neck verse'. Many criminals learned the passage by heart while in jail and so were able to read the words at their trial. Some accounts of this practice suggest that the condemned men were not actually reading, that the act of committing the verse to memory was, in effect, cheating. But this misses the point that they had learnt to read well enough to pass the test. They were, therefore, functionally literate. And the stakes could not have been higher, since functional illiteracy would have seen them hanged.

For many Muslim people today, literacy in Arabic constitutes a kind of literacy different from their literacy in other languages. It is about recognizing grapho-phonic correspondences, and so being able to produce the right sounds, when reading the Qur'an aloud (and the classical Arabic of the Qur'an is, of course, very different from any of the versions of Arabic currently spoken in North Africa and the Gulf States, for example). Such literacy practices are not confined to Islam: Latin has occupied an equivalent place within the rituals and liturgy of the Roman Catholic Church.

These might seem like special cases, but they point to the fact that literacy simply isn't a single activity. Think back to the high-school students and the professional historians: both groups were involved in literate practices, but in very different kinds of literate practice. For the professional historians, reading a text involved asking all sorts of questions about why it was written and what the writer was trying to achieve; for the high-school students, reading involved identifying and memorizing the facts (and accepting without question the authority of the text). These are profound differences that entail radically different conceptions of what it is to read, what it is to be a reader – and also, if literacy is seen as necessary for participation in society, fundamentally different ideas about what such participation might look like.

Questions of curricular entitlement, then, are not simply educational questions. They are questions about authority, about power relations, about the kind of society we want. The questions are fraught, subject to fierce contestation, because questions of knowledge are not neatly separable from values and beliefs. Clear evidence of that comes from the teaching of evolutionary theory.

Evolution and/or creationism?

As long ago as 1925, a Tennessee teacher, John Scopes, was prosecuted for teaching his high-school students about human evolution. The trial staged a confrontation between Biblical fundamentalists, for whom evolution undermined the authority of scripture, and an alliance of progressive forces sponsored by the American Civil Liberties Union.

That, at least, is how the story has usually been told. But it was also a battle for control of schooling, in which there were several competing interests: the state education authorities, who were seeking to impose a standardized curriculum; the local school boards, who wished to maintain their freedom of local decision-making; and the textbook publishers, who, interested in market share as a means of maximizing their profits, sought to exploit the conflict by discrediting their rivals.[3] Scopes was found guilty (though the conviction was later overturned on appeal). In many states in the US, the teaching of evolution has remained controversial, subject to legal challenge from those who have sought to present creationism, or (more recently) intelligent design, as alternative explanatory theories.

The argument is by no means confined to North America. In Saudi Arabia, for instance, the mandated school science curriculum contains one mention of evolution. The 12th-grade textbook contains the following statement:

> Nevertheless in the West appeared what is called 'the theory of evolution' which was derived by the Englishman Charles Darwin, who denied Allah's creation of humanity, saying that all living things and humans are from a single origin. We do not need to pursue such a theory because we have in the Book of Allah the final say regarding the origin of life, that all living things are Allah's creation.[4]

In the Iranian science curriculum, on the other hand, evolution is presented as completely compatible with Islamic belief. School students are taught about adaptations and natural selection. There are, of course, reasons for this difference between two Islamic states – reasons that are to do with the different histories of education provision in the two countries as well as to do with sharp differences between Sunni and Shi'a Islamic traditions.

In the recent past in England, too, there has been a furore about creationism and the teaching of evolutionary theory. It is worth retelling this story, particularly because of the light it sheds on the complex relationship between knowledge, curriculum and pedagogy – and because it reveals a widespread failure to appreciate this complexity. The trouble started when Professor Michael Reiss, director of education at the Royal Society, gave a speech at a Festival of Science in Liverpool in September 2008. Reiss said:

> ... about 40 per cent of adults in the USA and perhaps over 10 per cent in the UK believe that the Earth is only some 10,000 years old, that it came into existence as described in the early parts of the Bible or the Qur'an and that the most that evolution has done is to change species into closely related species.
>
> My central argument... is that creationism is best seen by

a science teacher not as a misconception but as a worldview. The implication of this is that the most a science teacher can normally aspire to is to ensure that students with creationist beliefs understand the scientific position. In the short term, this scientific worldview is unlikely to supplant a creationist one.[5]

In the course of the speech he acknowledged the fear, expressed by other scientists and science educators, that considering creationist views in a science lesson had the effect of legitimizing these views. And he made clear that he disagreed with this position:

When teaching evolution, there is much to be said for allowing students to raise any doubts they have (hardly a revolutionary idea in science teaching) and doing one's best to have a genuine discussion. The word 'genuine' doesn't mean that creationism or intelligent design deserve equal time. However, in certain classes, depending on the comfort of the teacher in dealing with such issues and the make-up of the student body, it can be appropriate to deal with the issue.

Reiss has been quoted at some length here because it is important to be clear about what he was arguing. This was not, however, how his words were understood. The BBC called him a 'creationism biologist',[6] while other fellows of the Royal Society demanded that he be sacked. Richard Dawkins' letter to the *New Scientist* described Reiss as an 'accommodationist', while also making the claim that 'the majority of Christians and certainly almost all Muslims' were 'naïve creationists' (thus revealing his ignorance of the Iranian science curriculum).[7]

Within a week, Reiss had resigned. The Royal Society's press release included the following:

Some of Professor Michael Reiss's recent comments, on the issue of creationism in schools, while speaking as the Royal Society's director of education, were open to misinterpretation.

> While it was not his intention, this has led to damage to the Society's reputation.[8]

Let's be clear. Reiss was not arguing for creationism to be taught in science, nor for teachers to pretend for one moment that intelligent design should be taken seriously as an alternative scientific theory. What he was doing was acknowledging the plain fact that students arrive in a science laboratory with widely divergent worldviews, some of which do not sit easily with evolutionary theory. And he was grappling with the problem that this fact poses for teachers – a problem that is both deeply ethical and intensely practical. (Of course, the problem disappears if you pretend that a curriculum can simply be delivered and that students are nothing more than empty vessels, waiting to be filled with the knowledge that the teacher supplies.) It was significant, perhaps, that Reiss's most vociferous critics were eminent scientists for whom no such classroom problems had ever arisen.

Part of what is revealed in this debate, as in all the other arguments about curriculum, are sharply different views about authority, about power, and about how learners are, or should be, positioned in relation to knowledge. For the fellows of the Royal Society, as for an increasing number of national governments, all of this is perfectly straightforward. Decisions about curriculum content should be made by experts – by academics or by government ministers and their advisors. The role of teachers is to deliver these curricula, and the role of pupils is to learn what they are taught.

This model depends on the premise that there is consensus (at least among the people making the decisions) about which bits of knowledge are the most important (because, presumably, these will be the ones that should be taught and learnt). Often, there is an assumption that some forms of knowledge are themselves authoritative, or powerful.

We, the authors of this book, happen to believe that the theory of evolution is the best available theory to explain certain phenomena in the world (how species survive and mutate, and therefore how human beings came to exist). But this theory, even among its adherents, is still a work in progress, still subject to contestation and debate. And then, of course, it is subject to different forms of contestation and debate among people who consider that Darwinian ideas are incompatible with their religious beliefs.

To pretend that this is not the case, or to dismiss those who hold different positions as simply wrong or ignorant, seems problematic to us for three distinct reasons. First, it amounts to a wilful refusal to acknowledge the simple fact that people disagree on these matters. Second, there is an irony in the use of institutional power to silence other voices: if the knowledge itself really were so powerful, why would this be necessary? Third – and most important – such a response is anti-educational: it stifles the debate that is, for us, the precondition of the advancement of knowledge.

What about the learners?

A curriculum, then, is generally produced by people other than those who are to experience it. Decisions about what to include and how it should be organized are made by governments, by academics, by the writers and publishers of textbooks, and perhaps even by teachers – but not by the students themselves. This might seem like plain common sense – after all, how could the pupils make decisions about the curriculum that they should follow? They don't know enough, do they?

This argument deserves to be taken seriously. School should challenge children and young people and enable them to develop, to think again and to think more about what they already know, to explore ideas and phenomena beyond their prior experiences. So it might seem reasonable that the curriculum – the plan of this

UNIVERSITY OF WINCHESTER *Rethinking education*
LIBRARY

learning – should be designed by more knowledgeable, more experienced others.

And yet there are difficulties with this position. There is, after all, a disparity here between schools and universities. In the latter, to a great extent, students choose not only which course to enrol on but also which modules to take, which options to follow. In higher education, the curriculum is largely *negotiated* between teachers and learners. This is not an absolute distinction, of course: particularly as school students become older, they are frequently allowed a measure of choice in the subjects they follow – but there is still a marked contrast. To what extent is the imposition of a curriculum on learners justifiable? How far should their agency be respected?

What complicates this issue is that it intersects with another aspect of curriculum. Hitherto the assumption has been that the same curriculum is planned for all learners in a particular society. In practice, that has never been the case. In more or less obvious ways, different curricula are designed for different groups of learners. Often, this is where there might appear to be an element of choice – a chance for the students to opt for a curriculum that matches their interests or meets their expectations. On closer inspection, however, these choices are – like the design of the curricula themselves – made by others on the students' behalf.

Where this is most conspicuous is in the academic-vocational divide, whereby, at some point in their educational careers, learners are taken on separate routes, provided with different curricula. One version is presented as more 'academic' – more intellectually demanding, more closely aligned with the disciplinary categories of higher education; the other with more 'practical', instrumental goals and with the sectoral categories of paid employment. Often, as the next chapter will make clear, this divergence of academic and vocational pathways is manifested in institutional separations – schools and colleges designated to provide one or other form of education. (Indeed, in the vocational sphere, the promise of 'education' tends to be superseded by the narrower offer of 'training'.)

To what extent is it the students who choose these pathways? Not much. To a very large degree, these choices are made by others, either explicitly, through regimes of assessment and ascriptions of 'aptitude', or through subtler forms of guidance. The very existence of the academic-vocational divide is a means whereby social inequalities are reproduced through educational processes (an argument that the next chapter will explore in more detail).

There are two simple points about the academic-vocational divide. First, all students should be entitled to learn about, and encouraged to reflect critically upon, the world of work as part of their education. Second, to see such learning as not academic is a misrepresentation, both of work (paid employment and other activity in the world beyond the school gates) and of intellectual activity (in school or outside). For, as Karl Marx observed, human work always has an intellectual dimension – it is never 'just' work – and that is part of what makes us human:

> What distinguishes the worst architect from the best of bees is that the architect builds the cell in his mind before he constructs it in wax. At the end of every labor process, a result emerges which had already been conceived by the worker at the beginning, hence already existed ideally. Man [sic] not only effects a change of form in the materials of nature; he also realizes... his own purpose in these materials.[9]

1 Samuel Wineburg, On the Reading of Historical Texts: Notes on the Breach between School and Academy, *American Educational Research Journal, 28*(3), 495-519, 1991. **2** ED Hirsch, *Cultural Literacy: What Every American Needs to Know*, Houghton Mifflin, Boston, 1987; *The Schools We Need and Why We Don't Have Them*, Doubleday, New York, 1996; *The Knowledge Deficit: Closing the Shocking Education Gap for*

American Children, Houghton Mifflin, Boston & New York, 2006. **3** Adam Shapiro, *Trying Biology: The Scopes Trial, Textbooks, and the Antievolution Movement in American Schools*, University of Chicago Press, Chicago and London, 2013. **4** Elise Burton, 'Teaching Evolution in Muslim States: Iran and Saudi Arabia Compared', *Reports of the National Center for Science Education, 30*(3), 25-29, 2010, nin.tl/evolutioneduiran **5** Luke Barnes, 'Misunderstanding Michael Reiss,' nin.tl/barnesonreiss **6** news.bbc.co.uk/1/hi/education/7619670.stm **7** nin.tl/dawkinsletter **8** *The Guardian*, 16 Sep 2008, nin.tl/reissresigns **9** Karl Marx, *Capital: a critique of political economy (vol. 1)* (trans. B. Fowkes), Penguin, 1867/1976, p 284.

5 Instituting difference: how schools reproduce inequality

'I raise up my voice – not so I can shout but so that those without a voice can be heard... we cannot succeed when half of us are held back.'

Malala Yousafzai

Children in school have always been sorted into tracks or streams – and often into different schools entirely. The new methods are not as overtly based on social class, race or gender as they used to be but the upshot is often broadly the same – far from fulfilling the rhetoric about opportunities for all, the education system too often reinforces social inequality.

When new students arrive at the Hogwarts School of Witchcraft and Wizardry, they are allocated to one of four houses by the Sorting Hat, a sentient, singing magical artefact. Placed on the head of each new entrant, the Sorting Hat determines where they belong. The criteria the Hat uses are not revealed, but it seems clear that heredity plays a part (so, for example, all the Weasleys end up in Gryffindor, whereas the pureblooded Malfoys are placed in Slytherin), as does aptitude (the Hat is able to make an instant assessment of each student's character and capacities).[1]

The Sorting Hat symbolizes a vital aspect of schooling. It identifies innate differences in individual students and uses these differences to place students in different institutional categories. The Hat might belong in the fictional world of Hogwarts and Harry Potter, but its function and mode of operation are representative of practices and beliefs that are centrally implicated in the processes of real-life schooling. Indeed, it is possible

Rethinking education

to construe school as the most important mechanism whereby existing differences – structural inequalities – in society are maintained, justified and reproduced.

How this works in practice involves divisions both within and between schools. There are significant variations in how the sorting mechanism works within different states and school systems, as well as changes over time.

Here, for example, are the words of the Norwood Report (1943), a UK government-commissioned inquiry which addressed issues arising out of the extension of secondary education to the whole population:

> Our point is that rough groupings, whatever may be their ground, have in fact established themselves in general educational experience, and the recognition of such groupings in educational practice has been justified both during the period of education and in the after-careers of the pupils.
>
> For example, English education has in practice recognized the pupil who is interested in learning for its own sake, who can grasp an argument or follow a piece of connected reasoning, who is interested in causes, whether on the level of human volition or in the material world, who cares to know how things came to be as well as how they are, who is sensitive to language as expression of thought, to a proof as a precise demonstration, to a series of experiments justifying a principle: he [sic] is interested in the relatedness of related things, in development, in structure, in a coherent body of knowledge. He can take a long view and hold his mind in suspense; this may be revealed in his work or in his attitude to his career. He will have some capacity to enjoy, from an aesthetic point of view, the aptness of a phrase or the neatness of a proof. He may be good with his hands or he may not; he may or may not be a good 'mixer' or a leader or a prominent figure in activities, athletic or other.
>
> Such pupils, educated by the curriculum commonly associated with the Grammar School, have entered the learned professions or have taken up higher administrative or business posts....

Again, the history of technical education has demonstrated the importance of recognizing the needs of the pupil whose interests and abilities lie markedly in the field of applied science or applied art ...

Again, there has of later years been recognition, expressed in the framing of curricula and otherwise, of still another grouping of pupils, and another grouping of occupations. The pupil in this group deals more easily with concrete things than with ideas.[2]

Norwood makes the confident assertion that innate differences among groups of learners justify the provision of different curricula and of different kinds of school – and that these innate differences map neatly onto differences in employment, in social role and status. What is remarkable about the Norwood Report is not the views expressed – the ascription of innate differences to individuals as a justification for stratified social roles goes back at least as far as Plato's *Republic* – but the clarity of its statement of this relationship between the segmented hierarchy of schooling and the division of labor within a class society. There is one type of school for the future hewers of wood, and another for those who are to be leaders of men. And what justifies this division is the innate differences in intelligence and interests that are ascribed to individuals. The system whereby inequalities are reproduced thus becomes entirely rational, justified by the already-existing differences that are to be found in the minds of individual children.

Selection versus inclusion

Things have moved on, of course, since 1943. In the developed economies of the Global North, there has been a significant increase in the number and proportion of white-collar jobs (though the repeated prediction that low-skill jobs would disappear has yet to materialize). In the UK, the increase in white-collar jobs was accompanied by a move away from the tripartite system that the Norwood Report heralded, where ostensibly different kinds of student were sent to different schools. So, from the 1960s onwards, more secondary students attended comprehensive schools – schools that were designed to cater for all types and abilities of learner. That, at least, was the aspiration.

We will come back to some of the factors that prevented the full realization of this comprehensive vision – factors ensuring that the system continued to reproduce inequality. Before doing so, though, it's worth making a point about the relationship between education and employment, between schooling and economic development.

It has become very fashionable for politicians to talk of the 'knowledge economy' and to make the claim that the route to national prosperity lies in improving the knowledge and skills of the population. As Tony Blair told the UK Labour Party Conference in 1995: 'Education is the best economic policy there is for a modern country.' The assumption that he and many other politicians make is that there is a causal relation between educational and economic improvement – that the former drives the latter.

The evidence for this is actually very weak. It does appear that the acquisition of basic literacy and numeracy by the mass of a population is a prerequisite for the economic development of a society. Beyond this basic level of educational attainment, however, the correlation between educational and economic standards is much more tenuous.[3] For individuals, education makes a significant economic difference; for societies, increased levels of education are much more a product (or a concomitant benefit) of economic development than a cause of such changes. So, for example, in the UK in the 1960s and 1970s, the arrival of comprehensive schools and the increasing proportion of the population who gained school-level qualifications and went on to university were not what led to the creation of white-collar jobs; they were, rather, a reflection of, and a response to, those wider societal and economic changes.

Those changes were to do with shifting patterns of employment; they were also social and cultural. The comprehensive school was intended to serve all the children in a neighborhood, responding to their different needs and embodying a sense of both universal democratic entitlement and community cohesion. It could be seen as a rejection of the old social hierarchies and divisions that were manifested in the Norwood Report and in the system of grammar schools for the minority and markedly less well-resourced secondary moderns for the majority. The comprehensive school in the UK, like the public high school in the US and Canada or the government school in Australia, was thus simultaneously about a different, more inclusive, model of education and a different vision of society.

Such a model was only ever imperfectly realized. There were unresolved debates about how comprehensiveness was to be attained – and indeed about what it might look like. Gathering all, or most, pupils together on one site seldom meant that all the divisions of the old selective system had been effaced. Just as American high schools used 'tracking', so British comprehensive schools tended to construct separate streams, dividing learners into different groups, ascribing different levels of ability or aptitude to them and providing each stream with different curricula.

The Norwood Report's application of the division of labor to schooling was not abandoned, merely modified. Divisions of class, gender and ethnicity were reproduced in the separate streams or tracks, and hence in the curricula that were offered and in the outcomes of schooling (the certificates awarded, the opportunities for further progression in education or employment).

Then there were questions about the pupil population. Should each school have an intake of pupils that mirrored the diversity of the wider society – a mix of classes and ethnicities, say, as well as of genders? If so, how was this to be accomplished? Should pupils be bussed into a school to achieve this balanced intake? Or should each school be a neighborhood school, drawing its pupils from the immediate area? If this resulted in middle-class schools and working-class schools, white schools and black schools, how did that sit with the notion of the school as *comprehensive* – as the site wherein social cohesion might be enacted? In more rural areas and in small towns, this debate scarcely impinged, since there was often only one secondary school within reach. In urban areas, on the other hand, the issue was real – and sharply contested.

But it was not only internal tensions and unresolved debates that undermined the social inclusiveness of the high schools, government schools or comprehensive schools across large swathes of the world; it was also the fact that such schools have always tended to exist in a mixed economy of schooling. There never was a truly comprehensive, fully inclusive system. There were areas where the old selective schools persisted. There were the private schools, offering their wealthy clients the privileges of exclusivity: small class sizes, large playing fields and the promise of access to the kind of cultural capital that only money can buy. And there were also, in many countries, the church schools, occupying ambiguous positions within the state system, with their own admissions procedures that offered the possibility of covert forms of social selection.

Almost since their inception, the inclusive ideal has also been subject to sustained attack from those who are ideologically opposed to the egalitarian commitments that it embodies. This rightwing critique has consistently understated the real achievements of comprehensive education, while at the same time exaggerating the contribution that the old selective schools had made to social mobility. In the UK in the 1950s, that heyday of the grammar-school era, most of the children of semi-skilled and unskilled workers who managed to get into a grammar school left with few, if any, qualifications, while only about five per cent of the children of unskilled workers who made it to grammar school emerged with two A-levels (the minimum requirement for university entry).[4]

Although the facts have never supported the demand for a return to a selective system, the critics of inclusive schooling have been able to draw on other resources to construct an abidingly influential argument. The narrative of a selective education as a means of individual enlightenment and empowerment has maintained its potency.

The story of individual advancement through education is much older than the story of the state's involvement in schooling: it is implicated in Romantic versions of the development of the self (the *Bildungsroman*) and in even older Protestant myths of individual betterment and/or redemption. The grammar-school narrative has retained such extraordinary power because it sits within a deeply embedded way of conceptualizing the individual as central to learning and development.

Despite both structural weaknesses and the vehemence of the ideological onslaught directed against them, the model of the inclusive school enjoyed broad popular support through the 1960s and 1970s. Comprehensive schools flourished in the UK, as did public high schools in the US and government schools in Australia. More recently, as the social-democratic settlement of the post-War years has been challenged by the growth of neoliberalism, school systems have tended to become yet more fragmented.

'Choice' and private schooling

The role of the state in the provision of universal education has been undermined by a range of policy initiatives, including low-fee private schools in the Global

South, charter schools in the US and academies and free schools in England. All of these have been driven by a commitment to market mechanisms, to forms of privatization and to reconfiguring the relationship between schools and the communities they serve.

We will return to the impact of neoliberalism on education in the next chapter. Here, though, it is worth drawing attention to the increasing emphasis on school choice. The emphasis on choice positions the parents and carers, as well as the learners themselves, as consumers; it reconstructs the terrain of schooling as a marketplace; and it emphasizes the differences between schools (since school choice is only meaningful or important if one school is regarded as more desirable, or appropriate, or simply better, than another).

It is precisely because the structures and systems of schooling reflect divisions in the wider society that they are able to function as a mechanism for reproducing (and normalizing) these divisions. How this works, though, is not quite as straightforward as the Sorting Hat. There are the overt, conspicuous ways in which money is used to buy positional advantage: elite private schools charge fees that only the very wealthy can afford – and thus a closed circle of privilege is sustained. Positional advantage is also bought in other, less spectacular, ways: parents pay for private tutors, or pay for their children to attend low-fee schools that are considered to be preferable to the alternative of state provision; parents move into the catchment area of a 'better' school. There is very clear evidence that school choice operates to reinforce existing inequalities in society – that choice is exercised differently by different social classes and that those with greater resources of mainstream social capital use it to their advantage.

The proportion of children who attend private schools, as well as schools that are to differing degrees independent of the state system, varies considerably across the world. In the UK, the figure has remained fairly constant for decades at below eight per cent. In Australia, on the other hand, it has risen considerably in the past half century, now standing at about 35 per cent. In North America, the figures are much lower: in the United States, five per cent attend private schools, and in Canada only three per cent – lower than the average for OECD countries as a whole, which stands at four per cent. These differences have an impact on both how inclusive state schools are, and also how inclusive they feel. In the Global South, too, there has recently been increased interest in 'low fee' private schools, which have been presented as the answer to the problems of lack of access to schooling and to the poor quality of the schooling that has been on offer (see Chapter 6).

Schools, too, have myriad ways to exclude those who are too poor to pay: for uniform and equipment, for specimen entrance exams, for school trips, and so on. For those who make it through the school gates, there is then an exclusionary force to the school's expectations of language, its rules of conduct and compliance. The culture of a school enables some students to flourish and alienates others. Some ways of speaking, of dressing, of interacting with others are valued; others are treated as undesirable or disruptive. None of these rules are socially neutral.

And then there is the concept of ability, or potential, and how that is deployed to normalize the sorting function of schooling.

The IQ test as Sorting Hat

As in Hogwarts with the operation of the Sorting Hat, so in the real world the divisions that are made and reproduced through the processes of schooling are made to appear as if they are merely responses to objective, already-existing differences between individual learners. Each learner is deemed to be the possessor of a fixed potential, an underlying ability. And it is the function of

Rethinking education

schooling to identify and then develop this potential.

Central to the operation of schooling has been the history of IQ testing and the view of intelligence that underpins it. Almost from its very beginnings in the first decade of the 20th century, the IQ (intelligence quotient) test has been founded on the following assumptions:

- that intelligence exists as a single, general property of each individual;
- that each individual possesses a more or less fixed amount of intelligence;
- that the intelligence possessed by each individual is objectively measurable.

The issue here is not just the speciousness of the assumptions themselves but the extent to which the history of IQ testing is implicated in processes of systematic exclusion and discrimination.

Devised by a French psychologist, Alfred Binet, the tests were originally intended for a purely pragmatic purpose – to identify those children who were struggling at school and who therefore might be in need of additional support.[5] Binet's emphasis was on the possibility of future improvement and learning. He recognized that intelligence was not a single, measurable entity (like height), and he was aware of the danger that the scale he created, which compared a child's chronological age with their 'mental age', was susceptible to being misread as a label of deficit and thus as a self-fulfilling prophecy. This was not his intention.

What happened, however, was that his ideas were appropriated by a series of American psychologists for entirely different, and much more malign, purposes. In the US, the Binet scale and the tests he had devised became embedded in a set of assumptions about intelligence as fixed and inherited and in a set of practices that had nothing to do with education and everything to do with social control. IQ testing was used to identify those who were considered mentally subnormal, and it was associated with attempts to prevent those who were thus categorized from breeding (since, if intelligence was indeed heritable and fixed, the subnormal genes would be passed on from one generation to the next, thus enfeebling the nation).

These ideas were not the preserve of a handful of eugenicists; they had practical consequences in the Immigration Restriction Act of 1924, which drastically limited the influx of migrants from southern and eastern Europe, and in the continuing oppression of African Americans. Mass IQ testing (particularly of 1.75 million US Army recruits during the First World War) produced data that were interpreted as proving the superiority of the Anglo-Saxon 'race' – though what a more rational reading of these data might have suggested was the direct correlation between poverty and low educational attainment.

In the US, then, the IQ test was used to provide support for racist ideologies and practices; in the UK, on the other hand, its primary significance was in offering a justification for the reproduction of class differences in education. The most influential figure in this story was Sir Cyril Burt (1883-1971), first as chief psychologist for the London County Council and then as professor of psychology at University College London. Though Burt has now been exposed as a fraud, systematically inventing the data on which his theories of innate difference were supposed to be based, his dogmatic insistence on a notion of fixed and measurable individual intelligence, and on the close alignment of intellectual ability and social class position, informed the system of segregated schooling that the Norwood Report had proposed.

The fad for 'learning styles'

Burt's research might have been discredited, but the conception of innate, fixed ability that he so vigorously endorsed lingers on. Sometimes it takes new guises.

Recently, there has been a fashion for identifying, and then catering for, different 'learning styles'. Some children are labelled as 'kinaesthetic' learners, others as 'visual' learners, others as 'auditory' (and so on). The teacher then becomes responsible for ensuring that appropriately stimulating activities are provided for each category of learner.

There are several problems with this, starting with the fact that there is no robust evidence that any of these types of learner actually exist (though of course it is true that particular activities might involve the use of a range of different faculties in any learner). The effect of the application of this theory of learning styles has been to encourage teachers to put children into different categories, and to treat the children in each category differently.

What compounds this has been the tendency to regard the different categories hierarchically, to ascribe different levels of intellectual ability to, say, 'kinaesthetic' and 'auditory' learners – and even to use these categories as a basis for deciding which subjects a learner is to study or which track she is to follow. And these individual ascriptions of learning style intersect with stereotypical assumptions made on the basis of gender, class and ethnicity. There is, for example, a marked tendency for working-class boys to be typecast as kinaesthetic learners.

Such judgements of difference become internalized: they become part of the way in which individual pupils see themselves. They become self-confirming, self-limiting prophecies. The student can all too easily assume that the content of a lesson, or the meaning of a concept, is inaccessible to her because she is the wrong type of learner.

It may well be that learning-style theory is merely a local and short-lived fad – though one that has left its imprint on the lives of many students. There is a sad irony in the way this theory has been used in schools, given that it has its origins in an argument against the assumptions that underpin the IQ test. Howard Gardner developed the idea of multiple intelligences as a critique of the overly narrow and rigid conception of intelligence that informs the IQ test.[6]

Schooling and gender

In myriad ways, schools both reflect and reinforce the constructions of gender that are enacted in the wider society – though it is also true that school can at times be a place where the oppressive and limiting ascription of gendered roles and identities is challenged and contested.

Still visible above the doors of board schools like those seen by Holmes and Watson, are the words 'Boys' and 'Girls' carved into the stonework. They mark not just separate entrances but a whole set of assumptions, both about the pupils themselves and about what an appropriate education might look like for each of these categories. For much of the history of formal education, gender differences have been made manifest in the subjects studied and the activities prescribed: domestic science (a label that itself revealed a complex of attitudes and practices in the gendered division of labor), needlework and netball for the girls; more prestigious forms of science, woodwork or metalwork, and football for the boys.

Schooling has tended both to exclude and and to impose identities, though in terms of race, class and (dis) ability as well as gender. Decisions about what might constitute an appropriate curriculum are informed by assumptions about the future lives of the students, about their place in highly stratified societies. What is deemed suitable for working-class girls has tended to look rather different from what is offered in high-fee private girls' schools: if the former emphasized the practical and utilitarian, the latter were more likely to devote time and resources to the cultivation of aesthetic sensibilities.

Likewise, the current panic about boys and literacy that is assailing many countries in the Global North is not so much about boys in general as about particular social classes (and particular kinds of literacy): the panic does not seem to be extended to the reading habits of the inhabitants of elite boarding schools, whatever their gender.

But it is also important to recognize that there is still a global gender difference in access to education – and that there are societies in which gender sorting takes sharper, more extreme forms. In recent years, the struggle for the universal right to education, particularly for women, has been both epitomized and championed by Malala Yousafzai, the Pakistani activist and youngest ever Nobel Prize laureate (2014). Chapter 1 referred to the Education for All movement and its concern for the Global South. The movement, which includes gender access as well as gender parity among its goals, reported in 2015 that:

> Girls, and particularly the poorest, continue to face the greatest challenges in accessing primary school. Nine per cent of children around the world are out of school. Among these, almost half of the girls will never set foot in a classroom, equivalent to 15 million girls, compared with just over a third of the boys. However, while girls are less likely to enrol in primary school in the first place, boys are more likely to leave school early.[7]

Although girls are more likely to stay on, they are less likely to move to the next phase of education. Gender disparities become greater in each succeeding stage of education; 66 per cent of countries have achieved gender parity in primary schooling, 50 per cent in lower secondary, 29 per cent in upper secondary, and only 4 per cent in further or higher education. For the poorest and most disadvantaged in the world, then, the issue is less about the ways in which gender inequalities are reinforced in school than about wider societal expectations limiting girls' access to education.

The Global South faces substantial challenges in achieving gender parity in education. Among these are entrenched discriminatory practices such as early marriage and early motherhood, gender-based violence, the priority given to boys' education and the gendered division of household labor. There has been progress: participation rates for girls have improved. But with this progress comes a recognition of school-based factors that can have a negative impact on the quality of education that is experienced. However important it is to provide sufficient school places and to insist on

The tyranny of judgement by results

In 1911, the British educationist Edmond Holmes, who had resigned from His Majesty's Inspectorate in disgust at his colleagues' lack of understanding of classroom experience, wrote a wonderful little book entitled *What is and what might be?*[8] The first half of the book, a searing analysis of the failings of the school system in which Holmes had worked, speaks directly to us across the intervening century. Holmes describes a system in which teachers spoon-feed their pupils, a system in which there is precious little room for genuine learning to take place:

> Why is the teacher so ready to do everything (or nearly everything) for the children whom he professes to educate? One obvious answer to this question is that for a third of a century (1862-1895) the 'Education Department' did everything (or nearly everything) for him. For a third of a century 'My Lords' required their inspectors to examine every child in every elementary school in England on a syllabus which was binding on all schools alike. In doing this, they put a bit into the mouth of the teacher and drove him, at their pleasure, in this direction and that. And what they did to him they compelled him to do to the child.

Holmes identifies the effects of a centralized curriculum, enforced through testing and through inspection. Within such a system, there is no space for creativity, no space for dialogue, no space to explore and exploit the interests and experiences that the learners bring with them. Schooling is a transmission process, driven by fear. What is also significant about Holmes's account, the right of all children to schooling, material factors – including overcrowded classrooms, untrained teachers and a chronic lack of resources – also need to be addressed.

The final two chapters of this book touch on two very different approaches to these issues. But for the moment let's return to the issue of assessment, and its often detrimental effect on schooling.

Five myths about assessment

If ability is the overarching concept that drives and legitimizes the educational construction of difference, assessment is the mechanism for applying it to the

---

though, is that he is writing 16 years after the ending of the system of payment by results. What Holmes understood, because he had seen the evidence in the elementary schools he had visited across the country, was that the pernicious effects of such systems of control lived on even after the systems themselves had been abandoned.

Within this system, Holmes identified the crucial effect of assessment:

> How did the belief that a formal examination is a worthy end for teacher and child to aim at, and an adequate test of success in teaching and in learning, come to establish itself in this country? And not in this country only, but in the whole Western world? In every Western country that is progressive and 'up to date'... the examination system controls education, and in doing so arrests the self-development of the child, and therefore strangles his inward growth.
>
> What is the explanation of this significant fact? ... The Western belief in the efficacy of examinations is a symptom of a wide-spread and deep-seated tendency – the tendency to judge accord-ing to the appearance of things, to attach supreme importance to visible 'results', to measure inward worth by outward standards, to estimate progress in terms of what the 'world' reveres as 'success'.

Holmes was describing an education system in which the tail of assessment wagged the dog of learning – and the echoes in the world of the early 21st century are chilling.

---

everyday world of schooling. Assessment sorts students into different schools, into different tracks or streams or sets, on the basis of what is assumed to be an objective measure of ability, or aptitude, or attainment. Assessment offers a window on the soul, a promise to reveal the truth about who individuals are, what they can do, or what they have learnt. And then, at the end of each stage of the process of schooling, it provides both a judgement on what has been learnt and the means whereby the next sorting exercise can be accomplished: it separates successes from failures, achievers from those who must try harder. It does this, moreover, with a studied impartiality, an objectivity that transcends the messiness of individual identities, interests and interactions, the contingencies of lived experience.

Increasingly, too, in this era of high-stakes testing and frenzied accountability, assessment is simultaneously a measure of individual and institutional worth: it tells us what each student has learnt (and whether their rate of progress has been sufficiently rapid), what each teacher has taught (and whether they have added enough value to what might reasonably have been extrapolated from their students' prior attainments), and what each school has accomplished (and whether the correct degree of pressure has been applied to individual teachers to ensure that they have each contributed fully to the raising of standards).

This kind of assessment is the cornerstone of the new technical-rationalist education system, since it is what enables inputs and outputs to be measured and compared, judgements to be made and action to be taken. It should be distinguished from other kinds of 'formative' assessment that are inseparable parts of the normal practice of teaching and learning.

Because of the centrality of high-stakes assessment in the modern education system all over the world, it is worth exploring five myths about assessment. To identify these as myths is to suggest two things.

First, that they are powerful and deeply embedded in dominant assumptions about assessment: they have become, in other words, common sense. Second, that they are, in important ways, untrue and unhelpful, obstacles that make it harder for us to arrive at a more accurate and adequate understanding.

Myth 1: Learning is linear

It has become increasingly hard to challenge the assumption that learning happens in predictable, identifiable and incremental stages. Increasingly, too, attempts are made to describe ever more precisely the progress that learners have made – and also to set ever more precise targets for their future progress. The scores, grades, percentages or levels ascribed to individuals are then aggregated to produce school-wide, area-wide and national data on children's learning. The attainment of literacy or of numeracy becomes inextricably associated with achieving a pre-specified threshold score at or before a particular moment in the process of formal education. The press and politicians are quick to make headlines based on the assumption that those who have not been awarded this pre-specified score are therefore illiterate and/or innumerate.

Yet this is, fundamentally, not true. Learning is a much messier, more complicated business than a linear scale of levels or grades would suggest. What happens day by day in the classroom depends on factors other than the learners' existing or target grades or scores: it depends on their interests and experiences beyond school, and whether they are enabled to make connections between these interests and experiences and the school curriculum. It depends on the learners' motivation. Even within subjects, such as mathematics, where the linear progression of learning seems more possible, students' understanding of, say, number – of arithmetical operations and concepts – can be at a markedly different stage of development from their understanding of shape, space and measure – of geometry – or of questions of probability.

Within subjects such as English, where development more obviously involves social and emotional aspects and orientations as well as intellectual processes, and where students' development as speakers and listeners does not bear any simple or constant relation to their development as readers and writers, it is far from clear that the attempt to place their progress at a single point on a linear scale is either meaningful or educationally justifiable.

This is a bad case of reification, more infectious and far more damaging than most communicable diseases. Test data that could only, at best, give some broad indication of a child's progress have been transformed into things, as if test scores or grades had the same solidity and materiality as, say, shoe size. In English schools you encounter with wearying regularity children who announce that they 'are' a level six, or a level three (the former with pride verging on smugness, the latter with an air of resignation, a meek acceptance that literacy, or even learning, is not really their thing). Even more worryingly, the reification process has affected the way that teachers talk about their pupils – so that 'she's a level five' or 'he's a level four' are now not so much shorthand expressions, standing for more complicated pictures of a student's development, as bald statements of fact.

Myth 2: Learning is context-independent

Closely linked to the myth of linearity is the idea that learning happens in a vacuum, and hence that it can be measured in isolation from the context in which it happened. This is another aspect of the same reductive approach to learning, an approach that seeks to isolate sub-skills and then assess whether the sub-skill has been acquired without any reference to the contexts in which such skills might be used and developed. Once again, it is an attempt to sidestep the messy contingencies of real learning, substituting in its place the thin abstractions of the easily transmitted and easily measured.

Always and everywhere, classrooms are populated by real people with particular histories, experiences, cultures. Learning involves these people interacting with each other and with particular materials – with particular problems, particular texts, particular resources. The learning that happens in and through such textual encounters cannot be adequately captured without paying close attention to the shaping influence of these contingent circumstances.

'Everybody is a genius. But if you judge a fish by its ability to climb a tree, it will live its whole life believing that it is stupid.'

Albert Einstein

Myth 3: Learning is individual

This is the myth that is most deeply implicated in the history of schooling: it assumes that learning is the property of an individual and that learning happens inside a single learner's head. Plagiarism is the cardinal sin within the religion of schooling precisely because it entails a transgression of this article of faith that learning is the property of the individual.

With glorious circularity, we know that learning is individual because the assessment regimes constantly demonstrate that this is the case. Assessment, predicated on the common-sense assumption that learning happens in an individual's head, proceeds to provide opportunities for the individual to demonstrate this learning, in circumstances – such as the exam hall – where normal human interactions are absolutely forbidden, and then offers conclusive proof of the validity of the procedure by arriving at differential assessments for different individuals: to one a D grade, to another an A, and so on.

It is in such routines of assessment that the role of education as a sorting mechanism becomes most obvious. Assessment separates sheep from goats, high-fliers from also-rans, leaders from hewers of wood. It underpins the notion of meritocracy and sustains the illusion that social justice can be achieved through social mobility.

The myth of the isolated individual, the learner as examination candidate, filters out all that we know about the reality of distributed learning, all we know about learners as irreducibly social beings, situated in history and in culture.

Myth 4: The assessment of learning is objective and reliable

Governments' education policies as well as current schooling practices are based on the myth of reliable assessment. In the creation of this myth, one of the things that happens is that assessment processes assume a kind of autonomy, independent of human agency.

But assessment is always a social practice. It always involves the exercise of judgement. It is always conducted for specific purposes by particular people. Only in the most trivial cases is assessment merely a matter of measuring. And reliability comes at a cost: the more reliable a test, the less information it can provide about the breadth of a child's learning and development. There is, in other words, an inverse relation between reliability and validity.[9]

Myth 5: High-stakes assessment is vital for accountability

The argument here is not over whether schools should be accountable – of course they should – but over the role of testing in achieving accountability. The whole machinery of levels and sub-levels does not make it easier for parents and carers to find out about their children's progress; it is a barrier in the way of communication between teachers and parents, a professional jargon that is impenetrable to most lay people.

The myth that national assessment frameworks introduced accountability ignores the fact that other forms of accountability, in the form of parents' evenings and school reports, existed long before such frameworks. To make this statement is not to claim that such systems of accountability were perfect – they were not – but the imposition of high-stakes testing has done nothing to address their shortcomings. Parents and carers want to know, among other things, whether their children are happy. And there is not, as yet, a National Curriculum level or a test score for happiness.

There is also a massive problem in conflating the assessment of individual learners and the judgement of the effectiveness of teachers, schools or school boards. Most obviously, using aggregated test data as an accountability measure tends to leave much that is relevant out of the account: it ignores the particular contexts of schools and their communities, and it ignores all the other aspects of a school's work that lie beyond the preparation of pupils for high-stakes tests. Worse than this, such accountability measures always and inevitably distort schools' and teachers' priorities, encouraging an exclusive focus on those aspects of a subject that are to be tested (reading and writing rather than speaking and listening, say) and on those students who lie at the threshold of success.

1 JK Rowling, *Harry Potter and the Philosopher's Stone,* Bloomsbury, London, 1997. **2** nin.tl/NorwoodReport **3** Peter Robinson, 'Literacy, Numeracy and Economic Performance,' *New Political Economy,* (1998) 31(1), 143-149, doi:10.1080/13563469808406341. **4** JS Maclure, *Educational Documents: England and Wales 1816-1968,* Methuen, London, 1969, p 234. **5** Stephen Jay Gould, *The Mismeasure of Man,* Norton, New York, 1981. **6** Howard Gardner, *Frames of Mind: the theory of multiple intelligences,* HarperCollins, London, 1984. **7** nin.tl/unescodoc **8** Edmond Holmes, *What is and what might be,* Constable, London, 1911. **9** Robin Alexander (ed), *Children, their World, their Education: final report and recommendations of the Cambridge Primary Review,* Routledge, London & New York, 2010, pp 320-1.

6 Neoliberalism: education as commodity

'Do you train for passing tests or do you train for creative inquiry?'

Noam Chomsky

Standardized testing, international league tables, paying teachers by results and privatization: these are key features of the neoliberal model being applied to education in many parts of the world. And now education corporations are actively developing the model of low-fee private schools – 'Starbucks schooling' – in the emerging markets of Africa and Asia.

Atlanta, Georgia, seemed to be a shining example of the success of US President George W Bush's No Child Left Behind policy. Schools in deprived areas with mainly African American populations were showing hugely impressive year-on-year gains in the federally mandated tests of literacy and numeracy. Under the leadership of school superintendent Beverly Hall, a rigorous program of target-setting and constant review had been implemented. The test scores in each school were closely monitored by a team of deputy superintendents, all reporting directly to Hall. Schools that met or exceeded their targets were rewarded: all the staff – cafeteria workers as well as teachers – were given a $2,000 bonus. Schools that failed to meet their performance targets suffered the consequences. Principals were fired, and their replacements were encouraged to appoint their own teams of teachers. No excuses for failure were tolerated. Hall, and the Atlanta school district she led, seemed to provide proof that the federal government's policy worked. Tough managerialism with a ruthless insistence on the achievement of measurable improvements was transforming education in one of the poorest urban districts in the US.

But there was a flaw in the success story. If the increases in the test scores, particularly in schools in the poorest areas, seemed to be too good to be true, that's because they were. The spectacular gains were the product not of better teaching but of something much simpler: cheating. In 2011 investigators discovered that around 180 teachers and school principals had been systematically inflating their students' test scores, often for the best part of a decade. Faced with targets that they could not meet and with the threat that their schools would be closed down, as well as with regular public humiliation when previous targets had not been met, teachers resorted to telling their students the answers or altering what they had written after the papers were collected.[1]

These teachers were not, for the most part, venal or self-serving. They cheated because they felt they had to, to protect their students and their schools as much as themselves. They cheated because of the intolerable pressure on them to meet targets that they knew they could not achieve in any other way. Cheating was an inevitable product of the system in which they found themselves.

It would be foolish to imagine that such things happened only in Atlanta. The pressure that was applied to the Atlanta teachers, the relentless insistence on improvement and on meeting externally imposed targets, has become a dominant feature of the landscape of schooling across much of the world. It may be only a small minority of teachers, in Atlanta or elsewhere, who cross the line to engage in practices that are manifestly corrupt, but everywhere the effect is to deform educational processes, to bring about a malign alteration in values, in relationships, in identities.

The GERM (Global Education Reform Movement)

Since the 1980s, there has been a fundamental shift in how education is envisaged and how it is organized: in school systems and in how the aims of education are conceptualized, in how schools are made accountable and in how teachers' work is regulated, in both the practices and the underlying values of day-to-day school life. These changes, originating largely in the US and the UK, have become a global phenomenon – the GERM, or global education reform movement, as Finnish educator Pasi Sahlberg has called it.[2]

What has happened in education is part of a wider neoliberal reconfiguration, one that is political, social and economic. It involves a realignment of public and private sectors – a shrinking of the state and an expanding role for business in the delivery of public services; more than this, though, it entails a fundamentally different view of society and of the individual.

Within this neoliberal framework, education is represented not as a right, an entitlement, nor as a (public) service, nor even as a process, but rather as a commodity – a thing, to be produced, valued and exchanged in a kind of marketplace. If education is thought of as a thing, it follows that it can be measured, and that different versions of it can readily be compared with each other. And if it is a product, its worth will be an accurate reflection of the quality of work of those who produced it. Much of what has happened in education over the past three decades has been the institutionalizing of systems of standardization, measurement and comparison. These, the advocates of neoliberalism proclaim, will enable the consumers to know what they are getting and the producers to be properly accountable for what they are providing.

Standardization starts with the curriculum, with the specification by government of what is to be taught, sometimes even how it is to be taught. The degree of specification varies over time, and from country to country. But the trend is clear: the curriculum is too important to be left to local negotiation; central prescription is the order of the day. Within this model, the notion of standards is made to do a great deal of work. It is both the promise of minimum levels of acceptable performance and delivery and the assurance of standardization – the claim that judgements made in one place are equivalent to judgements made elsewhere.

More is involved than this, though, in that the rhetoric of neoliberalism is always about raising standards. Higher performance targets are set, and there is among politicians an unshakeable belief that this will, in and of itself, lead to an improvement in the quality of education. More will be expected of the producers, and more will be given to the consumers. The product will be ceaselessly enhanced.

The neoliberal model prompts other questions, however. Who are the producers and who are the consumers? And what, indeed, is the product? Let's start with the latter question. As earlier chapters have argued, learning is a complex, social process that happens in the interaction between people and between people and their environment. Learning, and hence education, is, by definition, transformative: it involves change. But these effects are not readily reducible to a defined product.

How neoliberalism deals with this is by crassly reductive oversimplification – and by the alchemy of assessment. Learning in all its messy unpredictability is reduced to a set of outcomes: levels, grades, test scores. These products of assessment processes, that are at best mere snapshots, partial indicators of the learning that has been accomplished, become reified. The grade becomes the thing itself, the end-product of the whole process of education.

Payment by results

It is the focus on the grade or test score that enables precisely the kind of managerialism that was seen in

Atlanta. And it is not only in Atlanta that the culture of target-setting and performance management has had unforeseen, and highly detrimental, consequences. In many countries, it has become fashionable to introduce a system of payment by results: to reward those teachers whose pupils achieve or surpass the targets that have been set, and to penalize those whose pupils do not.

The rationale for such a system is simple and seductive. It seems reasonable to provide an incentive for teachers to work harder, and even more reasonable to reward those teachers who are demonstrably good at what they do. And what could be a fairer or more objective measure of the effectiveness of a teacher than the grades that her students achieve?

In Atlanta, the system of rewards was not quite so individualized. Paying a bonus to all who worked at a 'successful' school indicated some sort of recognition of a collegial ethos – an understanding that schools depend on colleagues working together, and that the contributions of all staff are to be valued. In many places, though, it is the individual teacher who is credited, or blamed, for the scores of her pupils.

Such systems of reward are particularly unsuited to occupations and forms of work where there is an under-lying duty of public service. In the 1990s, there was an attempt to rank the performance of cardiac surgeons in New York and Pennsylvania hospitals. 'Report cards' – data on the effectiveness of individual surgeons and the hospitals in which they worked – were published. As a consequence, the surgeons became reluctant to operate on the patients who were most in need of treatment, since these were the ones who were most likely to die. The doctors actually carried out more operations – but on healthier patients.[3]

The sophistication of the metrics used to determine a teacher's effectiveness also varies. Often there is an attempt to take account of the pupils' starting-points – so that what is being judged is the difference that the individual teacher has made (usually known as a 'value-added' measure). The 'performance' of teachers is, in reality, much more complex than is allowed for in any of these payment systems – and all such systems tend to have the effect of encouraging the participants to game the system. If as a teacher you are to be judged – and paid – on the basis of your pupils' test scores at the end of the year, you might be disinclined to accept into your class a pupil who is known to attend school only rarely, or who has a reputation for being disruptive.

In any case, it is much more difficult to determine the effectiveness of an individual teacher than any of these systems acknowledge. With the cardiac surgeons, one might concede that there are more or less objective measures of the success of an operation – there is the straightforward binary of life and death. But education isn't quite the same as medicine. Test scores are, as Chapter 5 suggested, not things in themselves but only, at best, indications of the learning that has been accomplished. Then there's the fact that the impact that teachers have on their pupils is not so easily measurable: some effects may be immediately apparent, but others may not be realized for weeks, months or even years. And there's also the tricky business of establishing causality – what it is that a teacher does that enables a child to learn.

The assumption behind payment by results is that the students' test scores are the products of the teacher's teaching, and that it is therefore easy to establish which teachers are effective. But it ain't necessarily so. Studies of teacher effectiveness have shown that the same teacher can appear highly effective one year, with one class, and rather ineffective another year, with another class. And, indeed, within the same class, a teacher may inspire one student and fail to connect with another.

This is difficult for school managers and politicians to accept. It's common sense that good teachers are easy to spot – but sometimes common sense is a bad basis for decision-making, let alone public policy. As Karl Marx said, if the world were as it appeared to be, there would be no need for scientific inquiry. (Just because the world looks flat doesn't make it so.)

Just how difficult it is to establish a causal relationship between teachers' performance and test scores is indicated by recent research in the US state of North Carolina. Jesse Rothstein found that there was a very strong positive correlation between measures of fifth-grade teachers' effectiveness and the test scores that their students had achieved *as fourth-graders* (in other words, scores achieved before the fifth-grade teachers had even started teaching them).[4]

Nonetheless, the neoliberal orthodoxy decrees that teachers and schools are construed as the producers, responsible for the quality of the grade or test scores that are produced. This has profound effects on how teachers see themselves and on the work that they do. The emphasis on measurable outcomes – and the consequences that these outcomes have for teachers' reputations, their pay, their futures – means that this becomes the focus of their work. The higher the stakes of the tests, the more preparation for the tests crowds out all other aspects of their role.

Schools become more like factories, with every activity regulated and subordinated to the imperative of attaining higher test scores. And, as the example of Atlanta indicates, the pressure is greatest in those schools that are situated in areas of the most intense poverty. The accountability regimes of the 21st century are driving schools back into the anti-educational practices of the 19th century – which is when payment by results started.

Increasingly, too, the effect of this narrow form of test accountability, with each individual teacher responsible for the results achieved by her own class, is to drive a wedge between teachers, to undermine the collegiality that has often been the aspect of school life that has sustained teachers and enabled them to develop and flourish.

It would be a mistake to see this individualization of accountability as an unintended consequence of high-stakes testing. It is, on the contrary, a defining characteristic of the workforce under neoliberalism. In such a system, there is no place for teacher trade unions or professional associations – bodies that represent those old-fashioned virtues of solidarity, mutual support and collective responsibility.

Teachers, like people working for Amazon or McDonald's, are subject to a regime of surveillance and performance management, their individual outputs recorded, scrutinized and endlessly compared against targets – and against the performance of their peers. As Margaret Thatcher, former British prime minister and early crusader for neoliberal values, said, 'There's no such thing as society.'

Australia provides a model of this accountability system in operation. The *My School* website provides details of every school in Australia. Data are presented on the pupils' performance in literacy and numeracy tests over the past seven years, and how these results compare with schools that are deemed to be similar. The site announces that it is:

> ... an extremely valuable tool for parents and carers, school leaders, school staff and members of school communities, as well as policymakers. As the site enters its fifth year, it is routinely used to help parents make informed decisions about their child's schooling, and contributes to both policy discussions and public debates.[5]

The process of education becomes one in which outcomes data serve as consumer information and in which the market values of individualism, competition and choice are taken as read. More than this, though, the outcomes data become the point of schooling: this truly is education as commodity.

It is also worth noting what this does to the students

themselves, how it positions them. They are neither producer nor in any very obvious sense the consumer of schooling. They are, in effect, reduced to a cipher: the test score stands in place of the student.

Who, then, are the consumers? Parents, who navigate their way through the marketplace, choosing among the available producers? Governments as investors in the test factories? Employers, selecting employees on the basis of their test scores?

What is striking about this is how little agency remains for the students themselves. The transactions of education, that might have been assumed to have the learners as the focal point, are carried on by others around them. Education becomes something done to them, not something that they achieve.

International league tables (and PISA-envy)

The focus on test scores is crucial to the neoliberal vision of education. It is what enables standardization and hence accountability across the system. If outcomes in the form of test scores are what counts, then it becomes easy to compare one student with another, one class with another, one school with another and one state with another. And test-based accountability has now become a truly global phenomenon, shaping local and national educational priorities and policies.

Since 2000, more and more countries have participated in the periodic PISA (Program for International Student Assessment) tests, administered by the OECD (Organization for Economic Co-operation and Development). These tests, in reading, mathematics and science, are taken every three years by 15-year-olds. The OECD then produces very detailed performance data, thereby enabling comparisons to be made between the performance of students, and hence of the education systems, in the different participating nations. Increasingly, the PISA league tables drive education policy. PISA envy inspires governments to look to higher-performing countries for solutions, ways of addressing their own schools' perceived shortcomings.

The assumption that informs such panic-stricken responses to any slide down the league tables is that context is irrelevant – that what works well in one jurisdiction can simply be imported into another. If it works in Shanghai, then it's just what Washington needs.

This is a pretty daft way of developing education policy. It simply isn't feasible to isolate one aspect of how schooling is done in one culture, one society and introduce it into a completely different culture and society. Schooling, as this book has emphasized throughout, is not a neat technical, value-free matter; it isn't reducible to outcomes or 'deliverables', precisely because it is embedded in a history of culturally specific practice.

This does not, of course, mean that it is impossible to learn from how things are done elsewhere – and indeed the OECD's own analysis of the PISA data has often been much more nuanced and well-informed than the responses of headline writers and politicians would indicate. But such careful responses count for little in comparison with a nation's place in the league table.

A further effect of the attention that is paid to the PISA tables in particular, and to high-stakes testing more generally, has been the narrowing of the curriculum. What is important is what is to be tested, and this becomes the focus of attention, of time and resources, while other aspects of curriculum, other dimensions of learning, become marginal. Literacy, mathematics and science figure prominently, become identified as the core of schooling; aesthetic and expressive aspects of the curriculum, on the other hand, are to be found only on the periphery, as occasional enhancements.

The process does not stop there. What literacy, math or science is – how these subjects are represented, what approaches are taken in the classroom – is determined by the test that is to follow. The higher the stakes, the more attenuated the curriculum becomes.

A rational interpretation of the data PISA provides might be that they reveal nothing more profound than that there is a fairly close correlation between economic development and education 'performance': the league tables of results consistently show a bunching of rich nations, with very small variations between them. But this isn't an interesting story, either for journalists or for politicians.

PISA has been, and continues to be, massively influential. There is increasing evidence of national governments altering their curricula to fit in with the perceived or anticipated demands of the next round of PISA testing. But it would be a mistake to see these changes as unmediated responses to the data that PISA provides.

When governments look to other 'high-performing jurisdictions' for tips on how to enhance their own position in the league table, where they look and what they seek to borrow are determined by ideologically informed readings of the data. So there is a tendency to look to Singapore, Shanghai or Seoul rather than the equally high-performing Helsinki or Alberta.

The East Asian education systems offer support for the neoliberal nostra of competition, testing and accountability measures, centrally controlled, prescriptive curricula and privatization. Finland and Canada, on the other hand, pose something of a challenge to neoliberal methods and assumptions: their inclusive public schools thrive without such externally imposed pressures, their teachers are trusted to make professional judgements – and their children make progress without having to deal with the stresses of high-stakes tests.

Furthermore, PISA is changing – and changing in a way that both mirrors and facilitates the neoliberal mania for privatization. In the early years of PISA, test design, data collection and analysis were all entrusted to international consortia of professional organizations. In 2013, the OECD awarded the contract for the administration of their tests in the US to McGraw-Hill

Education, the giant textbook and testing company. In 2014, the OECD gave the contract for developing the frameworks for PISA 2018 to Pearson, the largest education company in the world: Pearson will determine what is to be tested and how. It is worth looking carefully at the role that Pearson is now playing in education, particularly in the Global South.

Pearson: new markets and a new education model

In July 2015, Pearson sold the *Financial Times* to a Japanese company, Nikkei. John Fallon, the head of Pearson, explained the decision to sell the internationally respected newspaper that had been part of the Pearson portfolio for 58 years. The *FT* contributed less than £25 million ($40 million) to the company's annual profits of around £800 million ($1.3 billion).[6]

Pearson, with an annual turnover of nearly $8 billion, had made the decision to focus exclusively on education. This was not out of some sense of civic responsibility; it came from a hard-headed business assessment of where the profits were to be made. Its strapline may be 'always learning' but, as other commentators have suggested, it might more aptly be 'always earning'.

Pearson's involvement in education is nothing new. It produces textbooks and test papers, online learning materials and educational software and has a large consultancy operation. In the past decade, however, it has become a truly global player, with over 40,000 employees operating in over 80 countries.[7] It is in this context that the award of the contract for PISA 2018 needs to be seen. What Pearson is already doing – very successfully – is simultaneously influencing educational policy and providing solutions for the problems which it identifies (and thus creating opportunities for further profit-making interventions).

In 2011, Pearson appointed Sir Michael Barber as its Chief Education Adviser. Barber, who had been working for McKinsey (another education consultancy firm), came to prominence as head of UK Prime Minister Tony Blair's delivery unit, where he had developed 'deliverology', his uncompromising, outcomes-focused, market-based approach to public policy.[8]

In government, Barber was massively influential in promoting an approach based on the assumed superiority of the private sector, so that entrepreneurial innovation was to remedy the deficiencies and failures of the old, monolithic public services. He was, therefore, the perfect recruit for companies seeking to promote for-profit alternatives to public schooling. In 2012, Barber launched the Pearson Affordable Learning Fund (PALF) as a for-profit venture fund to support the development of low-fee private schools in African and Asian countries – particularly in high-growth emerging markets such as India, Pakistan, South Africa, Kenya, Ghana and the Philippines.

Pearson bought into Bridge International Academies (BIA), a for-profit chain with 400 schools already opened in Kenya as well as seven in Uganda, and plans for further expansion in Nigeria and India, with the aim of catering for 10 million students by 2015. What is significant about this venture is, of course, the scale – and it is this which drives Pearson's investment strategy. But equally striking is the version of schooling that it represents:

The strategic feature of BIA's business model is based on a vertically integrated Academy-in-a-box model (also referred to as 'Starbucks-style' schooling). This involves a radical stand-ardization of processes and methods, including curriculum and pedagogy, and a heavy reliance on data analytics and technology that enable the company to expand rapidly and achieve huge economies of scale. A scripted curriculum, providing instructions for and explanations of what teachers should do and say during any given moment of a class, is delivered through tablets synchronized with BIA headquarters for lesson plan pacing, monitoring and assessment tracking.[9]

What BIA offers is thus the apotheosis of neoliberal education: privatized, centrally controlled and outcomes-focused. Its cost-effectiveness is assured, not only by the economies of scale but also because of its unique selling point: who needs a qualified teacher when you can have a tablet?

Pearson, like other edu-businesses seeking to expand into hitherto underdeveloped areas of the market, have made large claims for the success of the low-fee private schools: that they reach the poorest children, those who have not had any experience of schooling; that they are more efficient than the public schools with which they are in competition; that they produce better results, higher standards.

There is very little independent research supporting most of these claims, and the most rigorous examination of the evidence available so far casts considerable doubt on them.[10] Rather than providing schooling for those children who have not had access to it, it would seem that the low-fee schools are operating in competition with the state schools, thereby further undermining existing provision.

But this argument is, in any case, not one that can be resolved by more objective evaluation data, since it depends on your view of what education is and what it is for. If education is a commodity, deliverable with the aid of scripted lessons and the rest of the paraphernalia of an 'Academy-in-a-box' and measurable through a few simple standardized tests, then there's probably nothing to worry about. Pearson will indeed be always learning – and always earning.

If, on the other hand, education that is worth the name is not reducible to these processes and these products, then we need to consider some alternatives to the goods that John Fallon and Michael Barber are selling us.

1 Rachel Aviv, 'Wrong Answer', *The New Yorker*, 21 July 2014, nin.tl/cheatingscandal See also Sophie Quinton, 'In wake of cheating disgrace, are Atlanta schools improving?' *National Journal*, 2 May 2015, nin.tl/atlantaschools **2** Pasi Sahlberg, How GERM is infecting schools around the world, pasisahlberg.com/text-test **3** David Dranove et al, 'Is more information better?', *The Journal of Political Economy*, (2003) 111, 555-588; see also Sandeep Jauhar, 'The pitfall of linking doctors' pay to performance, *New York Times*, 9 Sep 2008, nin.tl/paypitfall **4** Jesse Rothstein, 'Student sorting and bias in value-added estimation', *Education Finance and Policy* (2009) *4*(4), pp 537-571, and 'Teacher quality in educational production,' *The Quarterly Journal of Economics,* (2010) 125(1), pp 175-214. **5** Myschool.edu.au **6** nin.tl/Pearsonboss **7** Carolina Junemann & Stephen J Ball, *Pearson and PALF: The Mutating Giant*, Education International, Brussels, nin.tl/Pearsonmutating **8** Michael Barber et al, *Deliverology 101: A Field Guide For Educational Leaders*, Corwin/SAGE, Thousand Oaks, 2011. **9** Junemann and Ball, 2015, op cit, pp 19-20. **10** Laura Day Ashley et al, *The role and impact of private schools in developing countries: a rigorous review of the evidence,* nin.tl/privateschoolsSouth

7 Another education is possible

'Education is our passport to the future, for tomorrow belongs to the people who prepare for it today.'

Malcolm X

The neoliberal model of education may be dominant yet alternative approaches still exist. These are not just theories in the heads of educationists or experiments in other countries – they are being explored every day in classrooms somewhere near you by teachers and students who know that learning entails much more than passing tests.

Earlier chapters introduced some of the key debates around schooling. They have given examples illustrating the conflicts and dilemmas and showing how education remains contested terrain, fought over by governments and private businesses. There is no agreement about what knowledge is important, how learning happens, which teaching approaches work, or what the purpose of assessment is. In these debates, it has become common to marginalize the role of the teacher and to silence teachers' voices, particularly when these voices attempt to speak as one, through organized trade unions.

The neoliberal model of education has become the dominant one. It has affected how teachers and students see themselves and each other, how their work is conceptualized and how it is measured, and it has subordinated processes of learning and interaction to narrowly defined outcomes. But neoliberalism's even greater triumph has been to render its approach to education as mere common sense. It is this that makes it so hard to consider alternative values, practices and understandings of education.

Yet another school is possible. Alternative approaches

Rethinking education

to education have a long history – and they continue to exist today (and sometimes even to thrive).

Radical popular alternatives

That radical politics has tended to go hand in hand with a commitment to education is hardly surprising. From the 19th-century Chartists onwards, though, there has been a recognition that what is needed is not mere access to schooling but the development of properly emancipatory forms of learning. This is what informed the Chartists' demand for 'really useful knowledge' – knowledge that could serve the interests of the working class, that would be enabling and liberatory. The contrast was with knowledge that merely served the utilitarian goals of capital, was subject to the hierarchies of the established church and was constrained by existing structures of domination and oppression.[1]

Working-class education did not start with the board schools that so excited Sherlock Holmes. Rather, the establishment of state education might more properly be seen as a response to already-existing forms of popular education. Viewed optimistically, the board schools marked an extension of this provision; a bleaker interpretation would be that the State intervened to take control of schooling.[2]

In other parts of Europe, too, the 19th and early 20th centuries saw the development of popular and radical alternative forms of education. The Danish 'folk schools', for example, were established in direct opposition to what their founder called the 'schools for death' – the traditional, authoritarian education on offer from the nation's rulers. These folk schools, emphasizing democratic involvement and an orientation towards the world beyond the classroom, provided a template for similar developments in community education in Sweden.[3] More radical was the Escuela Moderna, an anarchist 'modern school' that opened in Barcelona in 1904. Although it was closed down by the Spanish authorities within a couple of years, and its founder, Francisco Ferrer, was executed three years later, the school provided the inspiration for other 'Ferrer Schools' in London, New York and New Jersey – and for other 'free schools' around the world.[4]

For the past 50 years or so, the municipality of Reggio Emilia in northern Italy has been a beacon of progressive practice in preschool and primary schooling. Starting out in the aftermath of the Second World War as a direct and explicit response to fascism, the project was founded on values that were both ethical-political and pedagogic: the commitment to participatory democracy was inseparable from the commitment to child-centered education. Learning in Reggio Emilia is understood not as the reception of already-established content but as an active, dialogic, exploratory process in which children are the co-constructors of knowledge.

In this tradition, great emphasis is placed on the 'hundred languages of children'. What is meant by this is an acknowledgement of all the resources of meaning-making that children have and acquire – not just the two languages (speech and writing) that are privileged in more formal, transmission-based systems of schooling, but all the semiotic means that are available: drawing, painting, pottery, photography, dance and drama.[5]

At the same time that the project in Reggio Emilia was beginning, an extraordinary experiment in democratic education was initiated in a secondary-modern school in the East End of London. From 1945 to 1955, St-George-in-the-East School flourished as a site of radically innovative practice.[6] The conventional hierarchical, authoritarian organization of school was abandoned at a stroke. In its place, under the leadership of headteacher Alex Bloom, there developed an entirely different version of education, one in which staff were fully accountable to the students and in which the content of the curriculum was something to be jointly negotiated, jointly created. The idea of the school as a community has become a cliché that often masks, or fails to mask, deeply coercive routines; at St-George-in-the-East, though, this idea was taken seriously, its implications worked through in day-to-day practice. And it worked.

Freire and education for liberation

In more recent times, the work of Brazilian educator Paolo Freire has been massively influential, throughout Latin America but also across the world. Freire's book *Pedagogy of the Oppressed* advances the idea of 'banking education'. His arguments go beyond critiquing transmission approaches as educationally weak, as he explains how such pedagogies 'mirror oppressive society as a whole', reinforcing the existing power relations.

Banking education achieves this through certain practices and assumptions.

1 The teacher teaches and the students are taught
2 The teacher knows everything and the students know nothing
3 The teacher thinks and the students are thought about
4 The teacher talks and the students listen – meekly
5 The teacher disciplines and the students are disciplined
6 The teacher chooses and enforces his or her choice, and the students comply
7 The teacher acts and the students have the illusion of acting through the action of the teacher
8 The teacher chooses the program content, and the students (who were not consulted) adapt to it
9 The teacher confuses the authority of knowledge with his or her own professional authority, which she or he sets in opposition to the freedom of the students
10 The teacher is the subject of the learning process, while the pupils are mere objects.[7]

As this suggests, the role of the teacher is paramount. Banking education reduces complexity by ensuring the power relationships run only one way. There is no question as to who is right or wrong, what is to be learned, or how it is to be learned. There is no scope for critical dialogue. The teacher's role is to control all educational events.

As Freire argues, this is dehumanizing for both teachers and students. The more the banking approach is used and accepted, the more passive students become. Criticism, questioning and drawing on the learners' own realities are in effect no longer seen as a valid part of the educational process. More than that, it inculcates a way of behaving outside school, where, just as in the classroom, one accepts the status quo, takes for granted the explanations by the powerful that this is the way things should be. The banking education model was perfect for past totalitarian regimes but is also being widely adopted in the privatized and highly marketized systems of today. What Freire did was to provide an alternative.

Freire's work emanated from his experiences teaching in Brazil. His arguments resonated with freedom movements and his published work has an enduring legacy as a revolutionary text (it was banned in apartheid South Africa). Although manifested differently from place to place, Freirean popular education has defining characteristics that mark it out as the polar opposite to GERM and the neoliberal versions of schooling.

Whereas the technicist, outcomes-driven approach of neoliberalism conceals its political orientation, popular education is overly political. It is an intervention aimed at the poor, the marginalized, the dispossessed, and its goals are never simply educational: it is about the emancipation of peoples and the egalitarian transformation of society.

Within Freirean practice, there can be no absolute distinction between curriculum and pedagogy, since dialogue provides both its method and its content. Education requires the critical analysis of the taken-for-granted, of the structures of domination and oppression that are so embedded that they come to seem natural;

and it has a clear, strong orientation towards action. For Freire, as for Marx, the aim is not merely to understand the world but to change it.

Freire's work has been hugely influential in Cuba. In the years following the 1959 revolution, Cuban society was transformed by a literacy campaign more effective than any other the world has seen. It is much more difficult to arrive at meaningful figures on literacy (or illiteracy) rates than newspaper headline writers, and even some educators, might have you believe. What is clear, though, is that the literacy brigades who worked tirelessly throughout rural Cuba in the early 1960s helped to reduce illiteracy to levels that would be the envy of the richest nations on earth.

In Cuba, about 2 per cent of adults are considered illiterate – as compared with about 12 per cent in the US.[8] This was accomplished without sophisticated materials or highly trained literacy specialists. What made the difference was the application of Freirean techniques in circumstances that were conducive to their success. Freire's emphasis on the dignity of the learner and on the vital importance of dialogue meant, and continues to mean, something different in the context of a society that is fundamentally committed to the values of egalitarianism and social justice.

Cuba was also able to export this success to other states in the Caribbean and Latin America – to Nicaragua, El Salvador and Grenada – because in all these cases the acquisition of mass literacy was inseparable from the revolutionary social movements within which these educational achievements were enacted.

Elsewhere in the region, Freirean approaches have not been so spectacularly successful; it would be a mistake, however, to imagine that nothing has been achieved. Even in less propitious circumstances, educational activity has been a salient characteristic of progressive social movements.

In Brazil, the Landless Rural Workers' Movement

(MST) has around 1,800 schools for 200,000 children. It has developed its own (Freirean) approach to teacher education: when landless groups acquire land, they elect someone to become a teacher. That person then attends the MST residential course, where students conduct research into their own communities, find out what education is required and negotiate an appropriate curriculum.[9]

Elsewhere in Latin America, social movements have developed similarly impressive educational work. In Argentina, there is the Popular University of the Mothers of the Plaza de Mayo; in Colombia, the Universidad Campesina (Peasants' University). In Ecuador, the Confederation of Indigenous Nationalities of Ecuador runs nearly 3,000 schools based on a model of community participation and has developed the Intercultural University for Indigenous Nationalities and Peoples. Better known still, perhaps, is the work of the Zapatistas in Chiapas, Mexico, where the Rebellious and Autonomous Zapatista Education System for National Liberation has been established. In such versions of schooling, reading the word is inseparable from reading the world.[10]

All of the examples in this chapter are important in and of themselves. They constitute real achievements, often in the most adverse circumstances. They are necessarily specific to their own localities: fundamental to the democratic values that inform these projects is an attentiveness to local needs, priorities and experiences. As such, they would not be easily replicated everywhere.

This puts such initiatives, of course, at the opposite pole from transnational edu-businesses such as Pearson, which are primarily interested in maximizing profits through 'scalability', replicating what is done in one place across different sites, countries and continents, in much the same way as the British Empire did in the 19th century.

In 2007 the Church Land Programme (CLP) offered Abahlali baseMjondolo and the Rural Network, two poor people's movements working in KwaZulu-Natal, a chance to elect two members each to attend the University of KwaZuluNatal in Pietermaritzburg. Abahlali baseMjondolo is a shack dwellers' movement founded in Durban and the Rural Network is an alliance of rural community organizations. The university program is an attempt to keep open a space for teaching and learning premised on liberatory assumptions.

Living Learning is neither an academic program nor a university degree – it is a space for reflecting on what it means to be part of two realities that are separate and often opposed. It tries to make it possible for activists to step into a formal university – which is mostly a machine for creating and sustaining inequality – without stepping out of a 'living politics'. At the end of the year the students from these movements wondered if it would be worth talking about 'achieving the "Universal University" – invading the academic one in order for it to benefit the people'.

In contrast to formal education, the Living Learning participants envisage a second kind of education, a 'liberating education that starts with the people's struggles to be fully human'. Yet things are not so simple.

There is also a third kind of education that appears progressive because it speaks the language of social justice rather than private profit. But instead of listening to the people, this education aims to discipline communities and even movements into becoming 'stakeholders' in 'service delivery'. It denies the thinking and experience in communities and movements – 'when an outsider comes, with their own language and culture and agenda, they can miss all the ideas that the people actually have'. This is a serious problem because 'the people are the ones who know about their situation'. And in such approaches, the suffering of the poor is often blamed on their ignorance rather than the system that oppresses them.[11]

Different schooling, different society

There is, nonetheless, a sense in which the instances of radical, popular, democratic practice have a meaning beyond themselves. They are instances of 'prefigurative practice'.[12] They show that other ways of doing school are possible, not in some far-distant future but now. They remind us that neoliberalism's version of education is not the only one, that other attitudes to learning and to learners are worth exploring. These alternative versions of education arise out of, and are embedded in, a different vision of society: one in which social relations are not determined by market values but by human values. They offer a different, much more direct and democratic version of accountability.

This chapter has focused less narrowly on schools than in the earlier parts of the book. Some of the examples (such as the work of the literacy brigades in Cuba or the Living Learning project in South Africa) are about adult education. All of the examples involve a different relationship between school and community, between school learning and out-of-school learning, between reading the word and reading the world. All challenge the notion that school learning and school curricula are neatly separate from lived experience. All are, in this, part of a rich tradition of progressive education that can be traced back to the early 20th-century American educator, John Dewey.

There is much to be learnt from this progressive tradition – the same tradition that the neoliberals have attack so vehemently because it continues to represent a threat to the authoritarian counter-revolution that they seek to accomplish. Dewey's emphasis on the importance of experience – the practical experience of the learner – points to the importance of those subjects or areas of the curriculum that most conspicuously provide opportunities for learning by doing. More than this, though, the Deweyan emphasis on experience as central to learning calls into question the facile acceptance of a transmission model of teaching, as if all that were involved in educational processes was the inculcation, through rote learning, of a series of facts.[13]

The examples of progressive practice – from Reggio Emilia to Cuba, from St-George-in-the-East to the Zapatistas – certainly help us question the commodified commonsense of neoliberalism. Yet they can seem impossibly distant from the everyday realities of mainstream schooling. They can thus encourage the view that, other than in these exotic pockets of resistance, neoliberalism has won and outcomes-based, market-driven education is the only game in town. But that view would be wrong – and the reason why lies in the creativity of ordinary classrooms.

The creativity of ordinary classrooms

Absolutely fundamental to the success of the neoliberal version of schooling has been its capacity to affect how things are seen. In focusing attention on what is most easily measurable and commodifiable, it has rendered invisible everything that lies outside its tunnel vision.

For this reason, a vital task for those holding out a vision of another kind of education is to make visible those practices and aspects of practice that the dominant neoliberal discourses of education policy have sought to efface. These more humane ways of doing school can still be found, even within systems of schooling that are governed by regimes of surveillance and test-based accountability, by commodification and privatization. The *Cultures in Contact* project described in Chapter 2, or the 'transformed' school visited in Chapter 3, are indications of what remains possible, even in contexts that are largely inimical to progressive practice. They are instances, however modest, of schools offering possibilities of development and emancipation.

Despite the best efforts of neoliberalism, classrooms – *all* classrooms – remain extraordinarily complex places. What causes this complexity? The short answer is people. Classrooms are full of students, teachers and sometimes other staff. They all come with varied experiences, histories, backgrounds, abilities, disabilities, inclinations – even in a school that does not appear to have a diverse intake. The students are not clones of each other; they will have a range of aptitudes, personalities, interests which the teacher needs to work with and work on.

Classrooms are also busy places, with myriad interactions taking place, many of them simultaneously. These interactions are public, available to the gaze of other participants in the lesson and open to scrutiny by outsiders (parents, school managers, inspectors and journalists, all of whom may feel that they have a legitimate interest in what goes on). There is, moreover, no neat separation between the formal learning that is accomplished and the personal or social lives of teachers and students. Events in these spaces are unpredictable.

For all these reasons, the teacher's role is far from straightforward. Teachers need to become adept at interpreting situations, organizing learning and managing events. They need to be proactive, to know their subjects and their students, to motivate, facilitate, communicate, organize and plan. They develop the ability to know what is going on in all areas of the classroom (as if they had eyes in the back of their head). They become multi-taskers. They need to create structures, clarity and momentum.

These are not skills that are arrived at easily or quickly. Teachers learn and develop strategies over time; very often this is partially intuitive and based on what feels right at the time with a particular group. They need to seek advice from a range of sources. The immediacy of events and specificity of context means school colleagues are often the most available and credible source. Thus teachers are learning and developing their practice all the time through a form of what we would call situated learning. This situated learning takes place within the school community but it also includes wider networks – professional associations and trade unions – that are both a source of professional learning and development and a vital means of resisting the neoliberal tide.

Classrooms are rich in interaction. This manifests itself in many ways. Teachers have to frame, explain, present. This could be to the whole class, smaller groups or individuals. Students ask questions of the teacher and of each other. Students need to develop the social skills to make the best of the busyness of classrooms. For example, getting used to being one of many, learning to wait, finding other sources of help. Dialogue between participants is key to what is happening. The classroom is a site of joint activities, of joint endeavor; it is a collaborative community. In this busy and complex environment, building relationships with the learners is very important. Relationships cannot exist without dialogue and dialogue creates relationships.

Teachers and classrooms are often represented, in film and on television, in a very limited (and stereotypical) way. There is the 'teacher as a performer', entertaining the students as if they had attended the circus. There is the 'charismatic teacher', the 'authoritarian', the 'intellectual giant' who knows everything.

Classrooms are also often presented with students sitting in rows facing the teacher. Even with the recent rise of 'reality' TV situated within schools, the work is highly edited, focusing on 'entertaining' highlights (such as misbehavior). The whole of a school week is captured in a 60-minute episode. The filmmakers tend to foreground a teacher-centered transmission approach to learning with the implicit power relations this requires.

If in today's classrooms, under the pressure of high-stakes testing, there is a fair amount of what Vygotsky called 'empty verbalism', there is also a great deal else happening that is much worthier of attention. Classrooms remain rich sites of cultural production. The work that teachers do is much more complex than the official script might suggest. And, even in the unfavorable context of an obsessive concern with measured outcomes, the everyday world of classrooms is one in which learners work together in complex acts of meaning-making.

Noticing these unremarkable and largely unremarked processes is vital: this is, in itself, a way of contesting the reductive version of schooling that neoliberalism peddles. It is also important that such processes – with pupils themselves as meaning-makers – are seen as work.

Classrooms are not mere sorting-houses, ensuring the appropriate reproduction of class difference (even if that is one of the functions that schooling fulfills). Nor are they merely places where children and young people are prepared for adult life, fitted up with the right skills to thrive in the new knowledge economy. Classrooms are places where work gets done, where transformations happen. What gets transformed is both the learners and knowledge itself. So, in an English classroom, *Hamlet* becomes a new text with every fresh reading (interpretation) of it, and every class that reads it is transformed in the process. And every time a History class explores the Russian Revolution, or the Peasants' Revolt, or the Mughal Empire, new history is being constructed.

Due attention needs to be paid to these processes that are evident in classrooms, processes that are both mundane and extraordinary. And, from this perspective, the fetish of knowledge as something that exists in hermetically sealed boxes, like the notion of the curriculum as the transmission of the 'best that has been thought and said', is hopelessly inadequate – and downright misleading. As the Bullock Report announced, over 40 years ago, 'It is a confusion of everyday thought that we tend to regard "knowledge" as something that exists independently of someone who knows. "What is known" must in fact be brought to life afresh within every "knower" by his own efforts'.[14]

Yet the emphasis here on the individual learner is also misleading – or at least provides only part of the picture. These efforts are accomplished socially, in the interactions between learners and teachers and in their interactions with the cultural resources at their disposal. Once we recognize this, we are in a better position to dismiss as hopelessly inadequate the notion that one could get an accurate picture of such learning by setting traditional end-of-course examinations in particular subjects, however 'rigorous' the neoliberals want to make them.

An alternative vision of schooling sees classrooms as sites of knowledge-construction. This vision is built on the reality of what already happens, day by day, in classrooms, but is neglected, almost invisible, because it does not fit into dominant discourses of accountability and assessment.

This vision:

- focuses on learning rather than knowledge, and acknowledges the messiness, unpredictability and elusiveness of the learning process.
- encompasses the irreducibly social nature of learning – an often uncomfortable dialogue involving competing voices, interests and understandings.
- resists the reductiveness of the neoliberal version of education, with its inputs and outputs, its testing and league tables, its production-line payment by results.
- knows that education is never merely a means to an end: it is an end in itself, a mark of what it is to be human, and to be valued as a full member of human society.

This vision is a starting-point that is rooted in current realities but it is inevitably no more than a beginning. The forces of neoliberalism are powerful, wealthy and well-organized. They have already done a great deal to deform the landscape of schooling, but theirs is an unfinished project. It is likely to remain unfinished because the Gradgrindian, bean-counting, facts-and-factory model of education is so profoundly unsatisfying for both teachers and children – and because it will not help build the more equal and sustainable world that we unquestionably need in the 21st century.

We will need to work together to resist these forces and to win broad support for our alternative version of what schools are and what they are for.

1 Richard Johnson, 'Really useful knowledge': radical education and working class culture, 1790-1848. In J Clarke et al (eds), *Working-Class Culture: studies in history and theory* (pp 75-102), Hutchinson, London, 1979. **2** Brian Simon, *Studies in The History of Education, 1780-1870*, Lawrence and Wishart, London, 1960; Phil Gardner, *The Lost Elementary Schools of Victorian England: The People's Education*, Routledge & Kegan Paul, London, 1984; Keith Flett, *Really Useful Knowledge and the Politics of Radical Education with reference to the working-class press 1848-1870*, unpublished PhD thesis, Institute of Education, University of London, 2002. **3** Sarah Amsler, *The Education of Radical Democracy*, Routledge, London & New York, 2015. **4** Judith Suissa, *Anarchism and Education: A Philosophical Perspective*, PM Press, Oakland, 2015. **5** Michael Fielding & Peter Moss, *Radical Education and the Common School: a democratic alternative*, Routledge, Abingdon, 2011; Loris Malagizzi, *I cento linguaggi dei bambini/The hundred languages of children (exhibition catalogue)*, Reggio Emilia: City of Reggio Emilia Department of Education, 1987. **6** Fielding and Moss, op cit, 2011. **7** Paolo Freire, *Pedagogy of the Oppressed*, Penguin, 1972, p 46. **8** Théodore MacDonald, *Schooling the Revolution: An analysis of developments in Cuban Education since 1959*, Praxis Press, London, 1996. **9** Liam Kane, 'Forty Years of Popular Education in Latin America: Lessons for Social Movements Today', in Hall et al (eds), *Learning and Education for a Better World: The Role of Social Movements*, Sense, Rotterdam, 2012. **10** Paolo Freire & Donaldo Macedo, *Literacy: Reading the Word and the World*, Routledge and Kegan Paul, London, 1987. **11** From Lindela Figlan et al, *Living Learning,* Church Land Programme, Pietermaritzburg, KwaZulu-Natal, South Africa, 2009, abahlali.org/files/Living_Learning.pdf **12** Carl Boggs,' Marxism, Prefigurative Communism, and the Problem of Workers' Control', *Radical America, 11.6/12.1*, pp 99-122, 1977/8, nin.tl/radicalamerica. See also: Fielding and Moss 2011; Amsler 2015, op cit. **13** Richard Pring, *The Life and Death of Secondary Education for All*, Routledge, Abingdon & New York, 2013. **14** Department of Education and Science, *A Language for Life*, HMSO, London, 1975, p 50.

Index

UNIVERSITY OF WINCHESTER 143
LIBRARY